Dear Friend,

We wanted you to have a book that combined the <u>very best</u> ideas in personal development, success motivation and sports training - a book that would guarantee you more success and happiness in your life . . . and in your future!

So here it is - The "WIN-WIN" BOOK. Enjoy it!

Haro Gefrung
Anthony Robbins

P.S.   Turn to the next page to see how fun and easy it is to use!

- ▶ **Browse through the book
  or look at the index in the back
  to find a chapter that you want to read.**

- ▶ **Each chapter is two-pages
  and takes less than 5 minutes to read.**

- ▶ **You don't have to read this book
  from front to back.**

  **You can pick any chapter you want ...
  whenever you want.**

*If you want to read a chapter about what happens
when you use this book, turn to Chapter 28.*

*There are 81 chapters covering 10 different areas
of sport and personal life.*

*See the Chapter Index at the back of the book
to get a quick overview.*

THE "WIN-WIN" BOOK

'Winning' In Your Sport and Winning the Game of Life

A 'Win-Win' happens when two people are playing a 'game' and they <u>both</u> win.

Professional sports trainers say that being an athlete is like being two people who are playing a game. One is the person you are in your sport - your 'role' self. The other is who you are in your everyday life - your 'real' self.

The two are constantly challenging each other, and when one 'wins', the other wins too! In other words, the great thing about being an athlete is that you can use what you learn in your sport to develop good habits and traits, and enjoy success and happiness in your everyday life!

GARO YEPREMIAN
ANTHONY RUBBO

Windom Publishing Co.
*1244 Snyder Avenue
Suite 133
Philadelphia PA 19148*

Copyright © 1997 Garo Yepremian and Anthony Rubbo

*The "WIN-WIN" Book™, The "WIN-WIN" Program™,
and "WIN-WIN" Camp™ are trademarks of
Windom Publishing Co.*

*All rights reserved
including the right of reproduction
in whole or in part in any form.*

*If you would like information
on Garo Yepremian's and
Anthony Rubbo's services,
or to learn about
income opportunities
in youth or adult motivation,
see page 20 in the back section.*

CONTENTS

The "WIN-WIN" Book is arranged in a unique, user-friendly format..

The Chapters

The eighty-one chapters are numbered in the upper right corner of each right-side page.

About The "WIN-WIN" Book

This section is located in the back of the book, directly following the chapters. The pages are numbered in the bottom outside corners, next to the page topic.

"WIN-WIN" 2
Here's How The "WIN-WIN" Book Works 3
How to Use The "WIN-WIN" Book 5
When to Use The "WIN-WIN" Book 6

Sharing The "WIN-WIN" Book with Parents, Coaches and Teachers. 8

Garo Yepremian 16
Anthony Rubbo 18
Writing to the Authors 20

The Chapter Index

The Chapter Index is located at the end of the book (starting on page 21 of the back section) for quick, easy reference.

- Garo's Guidelines -

*Don't settle
for just knowing the rules of the game.*

*Don't settle
for just knowing the right moves.*

*Go to the <u>heart</u> of your sport
and feel all the great emotions
that are part of your sport -*

*the fun,
the power,
the 'juice'!*

*Never settle
for anything less from your sport
. . . or from yourself!*

WHEN YOU PLAY WITH FEELING . . .

When you play with feeling . . . you are giving yourself the best edge you can have in your sport. Here's why:

Although your mind _knows_ the moves and your body _knows how_ _to make_ the moves, your feelings raise your _knowledge_ and _know-how_ to their highest potential. It's a simple fact that the more you play with feeling, the more effectively you play. So what feelings are beneficial to your sport? Optimism, enthusiasm, fun, boldness and humor are some. Does this mean that you have to be feeling all of these all the time? No, it simply means that you can bring them out *when you need them*. It also means that you can bring them to their max when the pressure is on. And finally it means that when you get knocked down, you can use the strength of these positive feelings to get right back on track.

How can feelings do all this for you? Well, when you feel threatened or face a challenge, your body reacts by making chemical changes that alert your muscles to attack the challenge or run from it. This muscle activity causes athletes to tense up, choke, judge poorly, lose concentration, give up, or even feel physically ill. When you can express your feelings naturally and strongly you can handle your challenges more easily. Instead of challenges making you feel tense, your positive feelings make you feel loose and confident.

To become emotionally strong, learn to express your *true* feelings in various life situations. Share your feelings with your family, with your close friends, with your teachers and other people whom you trust. This will free you up to let the natural *positive* feelings come out when you are in the game. *Imagine a future filled with constructive, positive feelings.*

Remember to get in touch with your *true personal* feelings (good or bad), and you'll find yourself expressing your most *effective* feelings when you most need them.

- Garo's Guidelines -

*Just for a moment,
forget why your teammates like your sport,
and forget that your coach and your parents
want you to play.*

*Now that you've forgotten about everyone else,
think about why <u>you</u> want to play your sport.*

*Once you're clear on that,
<u>your practice belongs to you</u>,
so play as hard as you want
and have all the fun that you can.*

WHEN YOU ARE PRACTICING YOUR SPORT 'FOR YOU' . . . 2

When you are practicing your sport 'for you' and not because you feel pressured by others . . . you are claiming your right to live your own life. This is a very important trait so let's take a look at it:

Always keep in mind that your sport is something that *you are personally choosing* to play. Don't ever allow yourself to be pressured into playing your sport. Don't go to practice because someone else wants you to go. Decide to do it only because it represents what you personally want to do, your own inner desire. That's how you'll get the most out of your practice and the most out of yourself.

Look into your true feelings about your sport. Why are you choosing to play? It could be that you like being with your friends, the feeling of competing (being in the action), the actual physical nature of the game (enjoying the moves and the skills involved). It could be that your sport is an enjoyable past time that gives you a break from other areas of your life, or a way to stay physically fit.

Your sport is not a job, it is something fun that you are doing 'for you'. If you think of it as a job, it will become a job. It's really that simple. What you call it is what it will become. Think of the effect that such an outlook can have on your life. You're either deciding to enjoy life, or to go through life feeling forced to do all those things that should feel natural to do. Look within yourself and find why you *want to* do your homework or why you *want to* do that chore. Make a friend and be a good friend because it is important 'to you'. *Imagine a future in which you are doing exactly what you want to do with your life.*

Remember that your best work comes from the feeling that you are doing it first for yourself. After that, be aware of how it may help others or make other people happy.

~ Garo's Guidelines ~

*Learn to be good
at your basic skills.*

*Learn to be better
at your basic skills.*

*Learn to be the best you can be
at your basic skills.*

*<u>Over-learn</u> your basic skills
so that they come so naturally
that you don't have to think about them.*

*<u>Over-learn</u> your basic skills
so that instead of having to think about them,
you can perform them to the max
whenever you want!*

WHEN YOU ARE LEARNING YOUR FUNDAMENTALS . . .   3

When you are first learning your fundamentals . . . realize that you are doing what every great athlete did to begin their career. It's how every successful person in every area of life began their rise to success. So let's talk a little about fundamentals:

There are two important things in playing a sport. The first is knowing the skills, the second is the maximum performance of the skills. Knowing your skills is about learning your fundamentals and building on them. (Maximum performance requires the mental, emotional and physical toughness that will allow you to play at your very best.) So what exactly are fundamentals? They are the very basic things you need to know to perform your sport. They can involve a swing, a particular form, a stance or movements that you repeat every time you play.

If you don't know the fundamentals in your particular sport, ask your coach or another knowledgeable person. Also, ask the best ways that you can work on them. True fun and satisfaction in playing a sport happens when you don't have to think about fundamentals. You know them so well that you can just enjoy the game and mastering higher challenges.

When you realize the importance of fundamentals in your sport, you will begin to see how every area of your life has fundamentals. For example, once you learn how to do a particular chore and strive to do it well, it no longer feels like a 'chore'. You will also realize that you don't have to be born with a certain talent to succeed. Look for fundamentals in <u>anything</u> you pursue and it will soon feel natural to you. *Imagine a future in which you can approach any interest or activity with the confidence that you will do well at it.*

Keep up that good work - good work that has its basis in the dedicated learning of your fundamentals.

- Garo's Guidelines -

*From one practice to the next,
keep track of what skills you're working on.*

*From one practice to the next,
set small improvement goals.*

*Let each practice represent
your own personal 'game',
and know what improvement
you have to make to 'win'.*

*With this outlook,
you'll naturally want
to practice regularly
to keep improving
your 'inner game'.*

WHEN YOU PRACTICE REGULARLY . . .

When you practice regularly . . . you are forming a habit that will create success in so many areas of your life. Let's look into this a little further:

Your sport is unique in your life in that it is something you are *personally choosing* to do <u>regularly</u>. You may think that this isn't a big achievement, but actually it's a great achievement. In fact, it is one of the most important things that a young person can do if they are in a team sport. When you choose personally to practice regularly, you are forming a solid success trait. Think about it. Success is a step-by-step process of reaching small improvement goals. Regular practice assures that you'll go through these steps confidently.

A regular and consistent practice program shows that you enjoy your sport so much that you can 'turn your enjoyment on' at a precise time, any day you choose, and for a set amount of time. It's at your fingertips. You can bring out that feeling of fun at a moment's notice or at a precisely planned time. This proves the ultimate feeling that you have for your sport.

The benefits of regular practice carry over into many important areas of your life, and probably the most valuable benefit is in your education. One of the worst feelings in the world is when a student falls behind in their work and feels like they can't catch up. It affects their whole life and can affect their entire future. Bring the habit of regular practice into your studies and you will stay on top of your schoolwork and enjoy your education. *Imagine a future in which you not only enjoy the successes of your life but also the regular everyday 'practice' that leads to success.*

Remember that regular practice and continuing effort will surely lead to improvement and success in your sport and in your life.

~ Garo's Guidelines ~

*The 'edge' is a magic feeling you get
when you're on top of your game,
when your fundamentals are so sharp
that you can push into new skills
and higher levels of performance.*

*As you become a better player,
don't forget to keep working
on your fundamentals.*

*As you become a great player,
don't forget to keep those fundamentals sharp.*

*Even the pros maintain their edge
by regularly practicing the basic skills
of their sport to keep them sharp.*

WHEN YOU KEEP YOUR FUNDAMENTALS SHARP... 5

When you have already learned your fundamentals and you continue practicing them to keep them sharp . . . you are learning how to develop an edge that will result in a steady improvement in your performance. Here's how it works:

The same way that skipping practice for a few days or a week will slightly lower your performance when you come back, regular practice on your fundamentals tends to slightly (but continually) raise your performance. Step-by-step you will improve and settle into higher levels of effectiveness. Once you settle for a while you will continue practicing until you reach yet a higher level. Occasionally have your coach watch your performance to make sure you are on the right track and that you aren't picking up any bad habits. Your steady improvement will continue as long as you keep your edge and practice regularly. Keep your fundamentals sharp and your technique will get stronger and you'll enjoy your sport more and more. Also, when you can rely on your fundamentals, you feel confident to explore new personal ways to improve your playing and discover more of your unique talents.

This will carry over into other areas of your life and you will realize that once you understand the basics of how to study, participate in class, do household chores, be a good friend, develop a relationship, etc. you can actually create the life you want by keeping those basics sharp and building on them. *Imagine a future in which you have learned the secret of how to improve any area of your life, whether it is your social life, personal life, career or professional life, etc.. You will be able to accomplish anything to which you set your mind.*

You know that by keeping your edge you will be rewarded in so many ways. So continue the good work you're doing, and keep those fundamentals sharp.

– Garo's Guidelines –

What do you do when you receive a gift?

You look at it,
you express your appreciation,
and you use it.

You are gifted.

You have been given natural talent in certain areas. These talents make it easier for you to achieve in these areas.

Watch your performance
for what seems most easy and natural to you
and work that talent to its potential.

Look at your gift.
Be grateful for it.
Use it.

WHEN YOU RECOGNIZE
YOUR NATURAL TALENT...

When you recognize a particular natural talent and develop it in practice ... you are beginning a habit that will make your life easier and so much more fun. Let's take a look at how this works:

When you recognize natural talent within you, you will begin to feel a strong desire to express that talent. It may be your speed, your arm strength, your quick thinking, your agility, your overall physical strength, or some other area in which you feel particularly talented. Rather than comparing yourself against other players' talents, strive to discover where *you* feel the strongest and begin working there.

Your coach can be very helpful in pointing out where you have natural talent. Once you discover what comes easy for you, learn to develop skills that support it. It is here that you will learn a very personal lesson about what it means to excel. It will be *your* personal excellence because it represents *your* natural talent. You can then look to your own high level of achievement and strive to bring your other skills to that same level. In this particular instance, you become your own role model. This is a very positive and self-empowering feeling.

Naturally, when you bring this idea into your school work, family and friendships, your entire life gets easier and more enjoyable. For example, you find the school subject that you most like, and use the feeling you get in that subject to enjoy learning other subjects. What is your best trait as a friend? Learn from it how to make yourself more natural in your relationships. *Imagine a future where you have built an entire life around those things at which you naturally excel.*

Keep up the good work, and remember always to let your natural talent bring you the satisfaction and enjoyment that you *naturally* deserve.

~ Garo's Guidelines ~

*When do you know you're giving it
'all you've got'?*

*How do you know
what your best really is?*

*You find your best and give your best
when you are challenged.*

*The quickest and easiest way to get challenged
is to have someone challenge you -
to compete with you*

*If you want to find your best and give your best
in your games, make it easy on yourself.*

*First find it and give it in your practice by
making your practice feel like the real thing.*

*Find teammates in practice who can challenge
you, and play to win!*

WHEN YOU BRING THE SPIRIT OF COMPETITION INTO YOUR PRACTICE ...

7

When you consistently bring the spirit of competition into your practice ... you get the most out of your practice and you are preparing for your games in the very best way possible. Let's take a look at how this happens:

What do you think of when you hear the word *practice*? Some athletes think that it's something that they *must* do, but that the real action is in the game. When you make your practice the *real* action, then you'll find yourself bringing a new edge to your games. In practice you have the opportunity to find your limits *and push your limits* in a 'safe' environment. So then in your game you are ready to perform beyond that point where most people have set their limits.

Practice is also the place to get tough. Look for the true spirit of competition in your practice. Play with and against teammates with the feeling that you are in an important game. When you begin to do this, it is then an easy next step to imagine yourself in a high pressure situation. So practice then becomes an opportunity to prepare for those high pressure moments you'll be facing in your games. The same way that an actor can bring up actual emotions and feelings in a role, you can actually bring up the actual emotion and feeling of competition so that when you're in a game, you're already familiar with the challenge of it.

In life, we are continually preparing ourselves (in one way or another) for important situations. When you prepare for them in a way that feels *real*, you will find a new sense of empowerment and enjoyment in your activities. *Imagine a future in which you feel a sense of personal power in your important activities.*

Keep up that positive spirit of competition in your practice, and bring out the best of yourself in all areas of life.

~ Garo's Guidelines ~

When you were a baby, you stood up and tried to walk . . . then you fell . . . then you got up . . . then you fell . . .

When you were a kid, you got on your bike and tried to ride, then you fell . . . then you got up . . then you fell . . .

Now you don't have to think about walking or riding a bike.

Why did you keep at it?

You wanted it, and somewhere within yourself you knew you had the potential to do it.

When a new skill feels uncomfortable, first know what it looks like to be good at your new skill, then:

1. Want it.
2. Know that you've got what it takes.
3. Practice it 'til you've got it!

WHEN LEARNING A NEW SKILL FEELS UNCOMFORTABLE...

When a new skill feels uncomfortable and you work through it . . . you are learning to train and prepare yourself for success in many ways. You are also learning the powerful lesson of *doing something right the first time so that it will be easier the next time.* **Let's look at this more closely:**

Think of one of the skills in your particular sport. Sometimes a fundamental such as a swing or a particular stance requires doing something that feels unnatural in the beginning until you master it. Then when you master it, it begins to feel more natural. At that point you realize that you will have much more success by doing it correctly. Because it feels unnatural in the beginning, many of us have the tendency to take a short cut which develops into a bad habit. Ask your coach (or someone knowledgeable) to closely watch your performance and point out any bad habits that you might have picked up. The greatest coaches believe in the idea of 'over-practice' - keeping at it to get it just right.

Learning new skills in other areas of life can also feel uncomfortable. Fortunately, you can look to people who have themselves gone through their growing pains to learn the same skill. Ask your parents, ask a teacher, ask a friend. You will be surprised how helpful this can be. A lot of people are worried about succeeding when the beginning stages of their success are particularly challenging. Make it easy - just ask someone you trust! *Imagine a future in which you feel confident in meeting the challenges of learning new skills.*

You know you have what it takes to be good in all areas of your life. So continue the good work you're doing, and be patient when learning those new skills. Your determination and confidence will bring you the success you desire.

- Garo's Guidelines -

Some skills feel harder to learn than others.

Some skills take longer to learn than others.

*Some skills require more dedication
to learn than others:*

*more time,
more effort,
more focus,
<u>more</u>.*

*The more it takes to learn a skill,
the more rewards you'll receive
once you've learned it.*

You will have developed:

*more confidence,
more courage,
more commitment,
<u>more</u>.*

WHEN YOU WORK HARD TO TURN A WEAKNESS INTO A STRENGTH . . .

When you work especially hard to turn a weakness into a strength . . . you are proving to yourself that nothing can hold you back when you set your mind on success. Here's how this powerful process works:

Have you noticed that there are certain skills that you can perform more easily and that there are some that are more challenging? Practice is the place and time to work on both. Keep up your strengths with the amount of practice required and focus strongly on areas where you need improvement. Strive to be well-rounded so that when you improve yourself as an athlete, you're improving your overall performance.

What happens when you work on a weakness is that once you begin working on it, you will tend to keep on working on it. You'll bring your skill in the weak area not only up to average, but you may keep at it and become 'above average' and eventually outstanding. In other words, you formed that habit of improving and you're not going to stop that habit just because you reached a certain performance level. Once a habit is in motion, it just keeps going, That's why you can become exceptionally strong in those areas where you are currently weak.

When you bring this into other areas of life, you suddenly feel unlimited in your potential. Many young people have difficulty in one or two areas of their lives and they let these areas make them unhappy about their lives. Now you know that you can turn the worst areas of your life into possibly the best. *Imagine a future in which you have no feeling of weakness in any important area of your life, and feel strong and confident in all areas.*

Keep up the good work on all those particularly challenging areas. You are forming a habit that will serve you well.

~ Garo's Guidelines ~

Timely Questions

What time does your practice begin?

*When do you have to leave
to get there by that time?*

*What do you have to do
before you leave?*

*What can stop you
from leaving on time?*

*Instead of starting with the goal
of being on time for practice,*

*start with the goal of
dealing with those things
that can stop you from <u>leaving</u> on time.*

WHEN YOU'RE ON TIME FOR PRACTICE AND FOR GAMES . . .

When you are on time for your sports activities . . . you are developing one of the most important traits a person can have. Let's look at what this trait can do for you:

Do you know one of the greatest challenges for adults in their everyday life? Being on time! When people are not on time they are simply *not keeping their word.* That's just <u>one</u> problem. Another problem is that not being on time may mean that they don't really *want* to do what they've agreed to do (at the agreed time). For example, if you were going to see a movie or a concert that you were really looking forward to seeing, you would probably get there early. Here's another example: Who do you think is more likely to be on time for work in the morning - the person who loves his work or the person who sees his work as *just a job*?

You have the chance to create a very powerful pattern in your life just by being on time for your practice and your games. You'll be saying, "I'm a person who keeps my word." "I'm playing because I want to play." "I'm serious about my sport". These feelings will show in your performance and your development as an athlete. If you rely on someone to bring you to practice, you can ask that they bring you on time. If you are ready well enough ahead of time, it will show your driver that you are serious about being on time.

In other areas of your life, you will find yourself becoming a more responsible person - someone who is very dependable. Dependable people are usually given more opportunities, more respect and more admiration than people who are not. *Imagine a future in which you are given the very best opportunities by people because they know that you are dependable.*

Show the world you're dependable and that you genuinely enjoy what you're doing . . . by being on time.

- Garo's Guidelines -

Okay, here it is!
Are you ready?
We're going to make a very important change!

We're going to change the word 'practice'
into a word that also begins with the letter 'p'.

Let's change it into a word
that means the real thing
Let's just call it <u>'play'</u>!

What's the difference?

Practice says 'have to'
Play says 'want to'

"I <u>have to</u> go to practice."
"I <u>want to</u> go out and play."

When you think of practice, think of it as play.
Think of it as the real thing.

Life just became so much more fun.

WHEN YOU DON'T FEEL LIKE PRACTICING AND YOU GO ANYWAY...

When you don't feel like going to practice and you go anyway... you are developing what many people think is *the* most valuable quality - Personal Commitment. Let's see how it works:

True personal commitment comes from enjoyment. When you enjoy doing something, you want to do it again and again. When you enjoy it so much that you make an agreement to do it, (such as when you join a team), you have made a personal commitment to it. Remember that your commitment was (and is) based on your enjoyment of your sport. When you don't feel like going to practice, you have the opportunity to create something very special - you have the opportunity to create *motivation*. A lot of people make motivation into a mysterious idea. Motivation is simply about why we want to do something. When you don't feel like going to practice, stop and take a moment to think what you like about your sport - the fun. Get in touch with your desire to go out there and have the fun of playing your sport. Put your desire ahead of anything that may be stopping you.

If you skip practices, you'll find yourself skipping in other areas of your life. If you make your practices, you'll bring your personal commitment into other areas. You'll reach goals in a step-by-step manner by doing the things you most enjoy. *Imagine a future in which your commitment is based not on what you 'have to' do, but on what you enjoy and look forward to doing.*

Admit to yourself how much you really enjoy your sport, and let your enjoyment be the reason that gets you to practice on those days that you don't feel like going. Your personal commitment will serve you well in all areas of your life.

~ Garo's Guidelines ~

Practice is the place for fun.

You can really 'go for it' in practice without worrying about real game consequences.

There's no real pressure, so you can pretend there's pressure to make it feel real.

There's no real competition, so you can create the feeling of competition.

There's no score, so you can score your own improvements.

In practice, you can discover so much about yourself, your abilities, what you really like to do.

Practice is your time to have your fun of learning your sport with your team.

WHEN YOU FULLY ENJOY PRACTICING . . .

When you fully enjoy practicing . . . you are getting the most out of your sport and preparing to get the most out of life. Let's look at how this happens:

Enjoyment is the most personal reason you have for playing your sport. Here are five questions and answers that will prepare you to discover the true secret of enjoyment:

1) When does enjoyment happen? *It happens when you like what you're doing.* 2) When do you like what you're doing? *When you do it well.* 3) How do you do it well? *By developing your skills.* 4) Why do you begin developing your skills? *Because you have the desire to play.* 5) How does enjoyment feel? *It feels loose, relaxed and alert.*

Now here's the secret to enjoying your sport. <u>Begin</u> with that loose, relaxed and alert feeling. In other words, enjoy it from the very start. Enjoy the practice, the moves, working on your fundamentals, learning new skills, working through challenges. When you start with this feeling, you'll realize to keep it going you have to develop skills, play well, let yourself go . . .and be in the moment! Then the cycle continues: the more you play the better you become - the better you become the more you want to play.

Take a look at your life - your friendships, your schoolwork, your family, how you are earning money, your interests, activities, and responsibilities. What would happen if you took this relaxed and alert feeling into all these areas of your life? They would get better and better and you would enjoy them more and more. *Imagine a future in which you have the best of both worlds - 'getting the job done' and enjoying it at the same time.*

Enjoy your sport and your life, and *earn* your enjoyment by developing the knowledge and skills that will bring you to the peak of your abilities.

- Garo's Guidelines -

As *an athlete, when you have 'attitude',
it means you have*
<u>*Confidence*</u>

*It's a look in your eye.
It's the way you hold yourself.
It's in the way you talk.
It's in the way you answer.*

*We're not talking about a 'bad' attitude here,
we're talking about a strong positive attitude,
a winning attitude, a playing attitude.*

*It's in the way you act.
It's in the way you react.
It's giving all you've got
without worrying about the results,
with no fear of failure.*

*Put attitude into your play
and into every <u>day</u>!*

WHEN YOU ARE CONFIDENT WHILE YOU ARE PLAYING . . .

When you are confident while you are playing in a game . . . you are expressing a trait that every great athlete has. Let's look at what confidence actually is:

Confidence is a feeling of certainty and sureness about reaching your goal or performing at a certain level. This feeling tells your body to be relaxed and alert so that it can perform at its best. Your confidence tells your teammates that you feel sure of your skills, and helps them to feel the same way. It also tells the opposing team that you intend to win, which makes for a better game.

Confidence is developed through practice, conditioning, and a positive attitude about yourself. When you go into a game, just let all your skills come out naturally. You know they're there within you. You've seen them in practice. The idea is to know you have all the skills you need to play great, and let those skills just happen. Confidence is not an out-of-control excitement, it is a firm, solid expectation that you will do well.

How does confidence work in other areas of life. Well, people like to be associated with a confident person, because they know that the person expects to do well. This adds to their chances of doing well. If they are also confident, it makes for a great friendship or team. So besides helping you do well personally in all areas of your life, confidence will also attract other people who want to do well. This in turn will keep you on track, because they will be expecting you to do your best. There is a saying that confidence breeds success. It does. *Imagine a future in which you feel strong and confident about reaching your goals, and have friends and associates who feel the same way.*

Remember that when you do your very best, it means that you are drawing on the strength of your confidence. So whenever you're playing, stay confident.

~ Garo's Guidelines ~

When those around you need to improve,
be their positive example.

When those around you are settling for less,
be the standard of excellence

When those around you are losing heart,
let your determination
inspire them to be courageous.

When those around you are losing ground,
let your focus
help them to forget
about winning or losing

and remind them to
<u>play their best</u>!

WHEN YOU'RE DOING WELL AND YOUR TEAM IS NOT . . .

When you are doing well and your team is not . . . there is something you can do to help your team, and learn a very valuable lesson while you're doing it. Here's what you can do:

Occasionally you will find yourself in a situation where you are doing well and your team seems to be lagging behind you in their performance. It could be that you are having an exceptionally good day and your team isn't, or it could be that a few members of the team are off and it's affecting everyone but you. Here is a great opportunity for you to experience the joy of helping others. Since you are not feeling the sense of worry or fear that your teammates are feeling, you are juiced to give your best. Remember that your enthusiasm is contagious, so keep it up and show your teammates that they can lean on your energy and use your enthusiasm to get them focused and back on track. It is in this situation that you are also expressing basic leadership traits.

Helping others often means giving something that you have to someone who doesn't have it. It could be intangible like confidence or peace-of-mind or even just a kind word to bring a smile to their face. It could be something tangible like food or money. When we realize that we are members of different teams in all areas of our lives, we strive to help wherever we can. Mom, dad, a brother or sister, a friend or classmate or relative - anyone can have an off day. When we help someone to feel better or to do better, it is one of the greatest feelings in the world. *Imagine a future in which you are naturally helping and supporting people with your unique positive traits and qualities.*

Keep up the good work, my friend, especially when your good work is naturally inspiring and helpful to others.

~ Garo's Guidelines ~

*In my sports career,
I've seen athletes warm up
in so many different ways.*

*Whatever method they used,
the purpose was the same,
and is the same for you:*

*to
calmly
and
confidently
remove everything
from
your
mind
other than
the confident playing
of your game.*

*Warming up is a personal thing.
Find out what works best for you.*

WHEN YOU WARM UP . . .   15

When you warm up . . .you are preparing for your best possible performance. Let's look at the value of warming up in your sport and other areas of your life:

Warming up is simply about making a transition from what you were doing and feeling *before your game* to the feeling you want to have *in your game*. In your game you want to be loose, relaxed, alert, focused and 'in the moment'. To get into this feeling, you can do an inner warm-up before or after your actual physical warm-up.

Here's how: Begin by putting your attention on different areas of your body - areas that are tense. Then let go of the tension. To *relax*, learn to take deep breaths . Fill your lungs and abdomen with air. Then hold it for a few seconds and release and feel all of your muscles relax as you are exhaling. To bring about *alertness*, <u>*confidently*</u> look at (or think about) the people, the playing area and the things that will be part of your game. To become focused, imagine a successful play. Then prepare yourself by sensing what you would be doing and feeling during that play.

You can bring this into other areas of your life. Just before an important situation or activity begins, do an inner warm-up. It could be for a school presentation, or to make a new friend, or anything that is important to you. Just think of what you want to happen and when you warm up, imagine it happening. This inner warm-up ability will get you through challenging events successfully in different areas of your life. *Imagine a future in which you're sure you will perform well in the most important activities and situations of your life.*

Let all your very hard work and practice show results in your game. You can do this by treating your inner warm-up as an *important part* of your game.

~ Garo's Guidelines ~

When you need to improve,

*let those around you
provide a positive example.*

When you are settling for less,

*let those around you
provide a higher standard of performance.*

When you are losing heart,

*let the determination of your teammates
inspire you to be courageous.*

When you are losing ground,

*let your teammates' focus
help you to forget
about winning or losing*

*and remind you to
<u>play your best</u>!*

WHEN YOU'RE NOT DOING WELL AND YOUR TEAM IS . . .   16

When you're not doing well and your team is . . . there is a way to improve your performance and get back in line with your team. Here's how you can do it:

When you find yourself in that unlucky situation where you are the only one who seems to be making errors and mistakes and generally not playing well, realize this: *Luck has nothing to do with it.* You have somehow broken off from your team's energy and you feel alone in your low level of performance. To get back, simply get 'out of yourself'. In other words, don't think about yourself and your own performance. Instead, focus on your team and strive to coordinate with their performance. The problem that a lot of young athletes run into is that when their performance dips slightly they give up a little inside. And if there is another slight dip, they believe that the downward trend is going to continue. Then they let themselves feel separated from their team's performance and begin to feel alone. The only way to avoid this is to simply stay connected to your team. Especially in this situation, think as a team, not as an individual.

Bringing this outlook into other areas of your life can save you from living an unhappy life. Too many people cut themselves off from rewarding friendships, relationships, and group participation because they've had an experience that makes them feel undeserving. When you are having a hard time, learn to draw on support from your family, friends, teachers and other people who are important in your life. *Imagine a future in which you can rely on the important people in your life when you need their encouragement or support.*

Remember that the people in your life are there for you. Let their good work continue to inspire you, and turn to them for support when you need it.

~ Garo's Guidelines ~

You're a winner!

*You've got that winning feeling -
loose, relaxed, confident, alert,
ready for anything.*

*Learn to hold that winning feeling
in your heart
and you'll find yourself
doing the things
that winners do.*

*Do the things that winners do
and you'll find yourself
having more wins.*

*Get that winning feeling
and make it
<u>a natural part of you</u>!*

WHEN YOU'RE SURE OF VICTORY . . .

When you're sure of victory and you have that total confidence in yourself and in your team . . . you're experiencing one of the very best feelings you can have in your sport. Let's look at what this feeling can do for you in your development as an athlete:

Naturally if a team is close to a win and they feel like they have the victory, they'll play with more confidence. What is actually happening is a total elimination of worry about losing. With that total lack of all fear and worry, they allow themselves to enjoy the game. If teams that are losing a game can psyche themselves into that same feeling and play 'full out' and enjoy the game, there would be a lot more 'amazing comebacks' in sports.

So remember that when people think being close to the win provides the 'juice', it's also the total lack of concern about losing that lets them give themselves totally to the game in enthusiasm and the pure enjoyment of playing. Here's the tip: When this occurs - when you feel that great feeling that comes with getting close to victory - observe the feeling, remember it and bring it into as many situations as possible - both in practice and in the game.

When you bring this great feeling into other areas of your life, you receive great benefits. Your work, family and school activities give you a heightened sense of enjoyment when you do them with enthusiasm. And 'juice' is contagious. *Imagine a future in which people in your life are more attracted to you and enjoy being with you because you express your natural enthusiasm.*

Remember that you can always turn on your confidence and your enjoyment whenever and wherever you want in your sport and in all areas of your life.

- Garo's Guidelines -

*Don't let anything
that you see, hear, think or feel
ever stop you from giving your best
and believing in your potential.*

Replace these statements

"They look better than us."
"They seem better than us"
"They <u>are</u> better than us."

with these statements.

"I'm giving my best effort."
"I'm striving to continually improve."
"I'm grateful for the competition."

*However it appears,
don't talk yourself out of a win.
Just keep playing the very best you can.*

WHEN YOU THINK THE OTHER TEAM IS BETTER THAN YOUR TEAM . . .

When you think the other team is better than yours . . you have a great opportunity to learn about the power of belief. Here's more about the power of belief:

When you think your opposing team is better than your team, you are naturally thinking that they have a better chance to win the game. Your thinking will turn into a belief and your belief will give the other team an extra advantage. Why is belief so powerful? It's because belief creates feelings within you that make actual physical changes in your body . . . and these changes affect your actions - your moves - the way you perform. Change your belief and you change your feelings and your physical readiness to perform well. For example, if you think it's going to take luck to win, <u>believe</u> in luck. If you think it's going to take a miracle to win, <u>believe</u> in the miracle. If you then win, you'll realize it didn't take luck at all and it wasn't luck that brought you the win. It was your belief that the win was possible. If they are a very good team, watch them, study them, learn their moves. If you lose, take what you learned and bring positive belief into your next game.

When you bring the power of belief into other areas of your life, anything becomes possible. If you believe strongly enough that you will thoroughly learn a certain subject in school, you will learn it, enjoy it and get top grades. If you believe that you are a good person and a good friend, you will make friends easily. If you believe that you deserve something that you want, your belief will move you toward that goal. *Imagine a future in which your positive belief in yourself brings you all that you desire.*

Remember the reason you do well (and compete well) is that you believe that you can. Use this power of belief along with your skills to reach your goals in your sport and in all areas of your life.

~ Garo's Guidelines ~

*In your sport,
as well as in life,
there will always be crowds
cheering and booing,
depending on which side you are.*

*Hear the cheers?
Hear the boos?*

*Your side of the bleachers
wants you to give your very best.*

*Their side of the bleachers
wants their team to give their very best.*

*If you give your very best,
it motivates the other team
to give their very best.*

*Make them all happy
and give your very best.*

WHEN YOU HEAR THE CROWDS...

When you hear the crowds calling out from the bleachers or the sidelines . . . you can use the sounds to energize your game. Let's see how:

Cheering, yelling and other sounds from the people who have come to see the game can be positive or negative. It's positive when it helps you in the game and negative when it distracts you and prevents you from putting out your best performance. If you find that it's difficult for you to pay attention to your performance, then it's time to work on developing better concentration skills. Learn to block out everything but what you're doing. In this way, the crowds act as a way for you to test your ability to focus, and can help you to improve in this very important life skill. If the crowds are cheering, you can also let their cheering energize you and inspire you to your best performance. How about if the crowd is booing? Here's a tip for that situation. Instead of hearing the booing, just feel the energy that the crowd is putting out, then take that energy and use it to energize your performance. This can be challenging, but whenever you see a great athlete who gets stronger in the face of booing from the crowd, this is what the athlete is doing.

In other areas of life, there are crowds that cheer you on when you do well. These can be your classroom, your family, your friends, or a special group to which you might belong. When you receive an award or any kind of recognition, it means that a crowd or an organization is cheering you. In your future career or profession, the 'crowd' might be your company or department. *Imagine a future where you are enjoying the recognition of your achievements from people who are important to you.*

Keep up the good work, and enjoy all your well-deserved recognition for your accomplishment in your sport and in all areas of your life.

~ Garo's Guidelines ~

*We have been given two things
in our sport and in life
that show us where we should be
concentrating our efforts.*

*They're called
'errors' and 'mistakes'.*

*1.
If an athlete ignores errors and mistakes,
their performance level gets worse.*

*2.
If an athlete gives 'a little' to their sport,
their performance level stays about the same.*

*3.
If an athlete calmly and confidently works
on skills to reduce their number of errors,
their performance level gets better.*

*Always choose #3.
Be the best athlete you can be.*

WHEN YOU MAKE AN ERROR . . .

When you make an error . . . you have an opportunity to learn more about yourself than when you are playing well. It all depends on your outlook. Let's look at this a little closer:

There are two ways that show that your confidence is working. The first is that you are playing well or reaching your goals. The second, more challenging test of your confidence, involves your reaction when you make an error. The amount of time you need to recover and to move forward shows how much confidence you have stored up within yourself. If a mistake or error requires too much recovery time to get back on track, it may mean that you haven't stored up enough confidence. So let's get back to working on your skills, your belief in yourself and your positive attitude. When you look at the 'greats' in sports and admire the magic of their confidence, you should realize that it was their mistakes and errors that brought them to that precision point in their performance. Errors are where they found their weaknesses so they could work on them and turn them into strengths.

This outlook on the value of errors will benefit you greatly in other areas of your life. How many times do people make 'mistakes' in their relationships and never resolve them. If you see a mistake as a guide to help you have a better relationship, what do you think would happen? All of your relationships - family, friends, classmates, etc. would just get better and better. And you will begin to see mistakes in school as a guide to better and more enjoyable learning, instead of just a lower score on a test or report card. *Imagine a future where there is no 'fear' of making a mistake, only the enjoyment of growing in knowledge and skill.*

Keep up the good work, and remember that errors are guides to your growth and development in your sport as well as in your life.

- Garo's Guidelines -

*All the great athletes know
that bad calls are just a fact of life.*

*They happen to everyone,
to both sides.*

*They're not something to be taken personally.
They're just part of any sport.*

*Use this fact of life to strengthen you
by getting
'bad call insurance'.*

*'Bad call insurance'
is being so focused on your 'playing'
that a bad call
won't throw you off balance.*

WHEN A BAD CALL IS MADE . . .

When a bad call is made . . . it can cause some young athletes to be distracted from their game. If the call was in favor of the other team, it can cause a feeling of frustration with the sport, and anger toward the official and the other team. Here's a positive outlook that will help you to handle this situation:

When you make an error, your team accepts it and keeps playing. When a teammate makes an error, you accept it and you keep playing. An official is also part of your game. After all, what would a game be like without an official? Who would make the calls? If he (or she) makes an error in a call, accept it and keep playing your best. Accept that it is not a perfect world (or that it's as perfect as human beings can be).

After your game, you can discuss the bad call with your coach or teammates. Learn to remember the plays and talk about them calmly and clearly. This ability will help you greatly in other areas of your life. For example, if you think that your coach or your parent is not being fair with you about something, you can look at the situation calmly and clearly and discuss it respectfully with them. If you find yourself in a similar situation in school, you can discuss it calmly and clearly with your teacher or principal.

This ability to take a stressful situation and look at it calmly and clearly will serve you well throughout your life. Since unfairness is one of the greatest causes of social stress, you're getting great practice in handling all kinds of people-related stress when a bad call is made. *Imagine a life in which you remain clear, calm and effective in the most stressful of situations.*

Learn to use everything to your advantage. Remember that the most challenging situations often contain the best lessons and help you develop the finest traits.

- Garo's Guidelines -

*There is only
one time you can
watch your teammates
play a live game,*

*one time that you can
watch all of their moves,
all of their great plays,
all of their errors,*

*one time when you can
easily imagine yourself
playing in a game
and realize exactly
where you need to improve.*

*That one time is when you're not playing,
and you're sitting and watching your team play.*

Take advantage of time on the bench!

WHEN YOU'RE NOT PLAYING IN A GAME... 22

When you're not playing in a game . . . you can learn things that you can't learn any other way. Let's see how you can turn 'not playing' into an advantage:

Think about it. The only way that you can watch all your teammates perform in a game situation is when you yourself are not playing. Use your time on the bench constructively by watching the various situations in the game. For example, watch the position that you would ordinarily be playing. Observe the player's stance, the way they move, their speed, their reaction time, their follow-through, their recovery after an error and everything about their performance. Imagine making the moves that they are making and successfully completing the plays. This is one of the most direct ways of imagining or visualizing a successful performance because you are actually watching players who are close to you in skill and who are wearing your team's uniform. Watch how your position works with the rest of the team and imagine yourself step-by-step coordinating your moves with the rest of the team. Sense where your skills need to be developed to be able to play at that high level of performance.

Instead of feeling left out, decide that you are choosing to watch your team - that you are removing yourself from the situation so you can observe it more clearly. In family life and other areas of your life, it's a good idea to occasionally remove yourself from the situation so you can see things more clearly. This will allow you to see all points-of-view. You'll be surprised to learn the true feelings of your mom, dad, brother, sister, friends or teacher when you take 'time out' to see them clearly for who they are. *Imagine a future in which you see life clearly, and are successful because of your clarity.*

Remember to use the time you are not playing to watch and learn from your team's performance.

~ Garo's Guidelines ~

You've won!

*Hold that winning feeling
in your heart.
Realize that the only way
you can get that feeling
again
is to win again.*

*Let that great feeling guide you
in your practice
and in your playing.*

*Be a winner on the inside
and you'll have many wins
on the outside.*

WHEN YOU WIN... 23

When you win a game . . . you are getting the message that practice, conditioning and a positive attitude really do pay off. Here's more about it:

When you win a game, you enjoy that great feeling of being part of the winning team besides *personally* being a winner. If the team you played ranked higher than you, remember your high level of performance and strive to take it into practice as well as into your next game. If the team ranked the same or lower, enjoy the win but be careful not to become laxed in your practice because you think you don't need to work so hard to win. Be realistic.

When you win, remember that your coach, the league, and your parents are helping to make this experience of winning possible for you. But realize that 'you are the winner'. Look at your teammates and realize that they are also all winners. Winning is what shows that a team is playing well together.

The *larger* goal of winning happens by first reaching *smaller* goals. Whether they're called runs, touchdowns, points, simply goals or any other names, there are the smaller goals that contribute to the win. In this respect, life is like a game. For example, you might want to learn about a school subject. Your smaller goals might be to read a number of sections in a book. The game is then 'the test', and a certain mark might represent 'the win' for you. A test is simply to show how well you have 'practiced' your own learning ability. Winning in a friendship also has the smaller goals of knowing more and more about each other (or doing more and more with each other). *Imagine a future in which you are a winner at the game of life because of your focus on the smaller goals of ongoing improvement.*

Always remember that when you focus on the inner game of steady, ongoing improvement, all the wins and victories take care of themselves.

- Garo's Guidelines -

We're all in this together.

Whether your uniform is
red, blue, yellow, green
or any other color,
your sport is the same.

Let's all be good sports.

On the personal side:

Whether our skin is
white, brown, yellow or red,
we're all people.

Let's all be family.

WHEN YOU `HIGH-FIVE' THE OTHER TEAM . . .

When you `high-five' the other team . . . you are playing an important part of the 'inner game'. Here's why:

Although you are competing with the other team during your game, there is a larger way to think about the other team and their meaning in your sport. When you `high-five' or shake hands with the other team after a game, you are saying that you are all supporting each other for a common purpose - to learn your sport and to have fun. A good thing to remember is that when the other team is giving you their best game, it motivates you to be your best - to reach deep inside yourself to find what you can really do when you are called to the challenge. For this opportunity you should be grateful, and the high-five is a way of saying, "Thanks for the game".

Whether you win or lose, this is something you do after every game, so treat it as an important part of the game. Don't do it because you have to or because the coach says to do it. Look within yourself and find out why *you want to* make this friendly gesture to the other team. In other areas of life, see the advantage of having competition. In school, you might enter a spelling, math or other kind of competition. Your ranking in the contest tells you how well you know the material and it can inspire you to reach your higher potential. Be grateful to your competition for helping you to find your personal best. Remember always that it is your enjoyment of the subject that is the basis for your involvement. Ranking high or winning shows how much you enjoy it. In career or professional life, competition is a fact of life. When you think of your athletic competition in a positive way, you'll bring this positive attitude into your future career, and excel. *Imagine a future in which you see everyone (even your competition) as contributing to your success.*

Keep up the good work, and continue to use competition to improve your playing and enjoy your life.

- Garo's Guidelines -

Your awards!

*Keep them
and
display them.*

*Look at them to remind
yourself that you are
a very special person.*

*You are an
'athlete'.*

*And you are a
'teammate'.*

WHEN YOU RECEIVE AN AWARD . . .   25

When you receive an award . . . you learn the value of being recognized for achievements and positive traits and qualities. Here's more about it:

At the end of your season, you receive an award for playing your sport. It could be a certificate, patch, plaque or trophy. This award says that you are considered a winner just for deciding to play your sport and recognizes the positive traits it takes to stay in a sport. When you put out your very best effort in your sport, there's also a chance that you will be recognized with a special award. Any sports award that you receive points to two important qualities - your commitment to developing traits and skills required in your sport, and your spirit of cooperation in using your talent, traits and skills to contribute to your team. The best way to accept an award is with humility and gratefulness for the talent you've been given and in a way that keeps you focused on future success.

Awards are important because what people think about you is important. In fact, some people believe that recognition is the most effective way to motivate them.

In your school life, you receive awards for you effort. In family life, you are recognized for your contributions. You will find awards in different shapes and sizes in your future career or profession. You will be awarded a certain position based on your skills and traits. You will be awarded a raise in your position or salary based on your commitment and level of performance. Life will be full of recognition and awards as you give yourself to worthwhile causes and goals. *Imagine a future in which you feel continually motivated because of the recognition you are receiving for your efforts.*

Realize how important people are in your life, and enjoy all the well-deserved recognition you receive from developing your finest traits and skills.

~ Garo's Guidelines ~

*The most valuable player
in the game of your life
is
'You'.*

*Take a moment
to remind yourself
of all the great things
that make you
an MVP in life.*

*When an MVP is chosen
after a game,
take a moment to
think of their own
great traits and qualities,*

and congratulate them!

WHEN AN MVP IS CHOSEN...

When an MVP is chosen ... there is a valuable lesson to be learned. Let's take a closer look:

The practice of choosing the most valuable player after a game provides a great benefit to both the MVP and <u>all</u> members of the team. The MVP represents the potential of the team. In doing the most for the team, they can be seen as the team's 'leadership' for the particular game. When you are chosen as MVP or recognized as 'the star of the game', you are standing out in the crowd - you are having your moment. But whether you are chosen or someone else is, the message is still the same - anybody has the potential to be their best.

How will this help you in other areas of your life? Well, we all belong to various teams or groups. Our family is a group, our classroom is a group. When a group has goals, there is usually someone contributing a little more than others - the group's MVP. Just like in your sport, the group's MVP may change from one week to the next. Do you want to be very valuable to your family? Look at the chores that need to be done in your home. These chores are part of your 'family game'. Be an MVP in your family this week by looking over the list of household chores and giving a little extra. Try it for a week and see how it feels. You'll find that when you give value to your family (or any group) that the value comes back to you. This is a law of human nature, and if you truly believe in it, good things will come to you. Naturally, your future career or profession will have many opportunities for you to be an MVP. *Imagine a future in which you are constantly striving for and often reaching your potential in the various groups of your life.*

Learn to see your knowledge, traits and skills in terms of the value they represent to a particular group in your life. Add your personal contribution to the efforts of others and make your life extraordinary.

- Garo's Guidelines -

You like your sport
so you spend hours and hours
to prepare for your games.

Since you spend
so many hours
<u>before</u> your games
in preparation,

why not spend
just a few minutes
after your games
to review them
and learn from them.

WHEN YOU REVIEW YOUR GAME... 27

When you review your game... you can build confidence and learn valuable personal lessons. Here's how:

The way you see yourself plays a big part in whether you are successful in life. If you see yourself as a successful person, you will act successful and people will treat you the way that successful people are treated. If you think you're a likable person, you will find a lot of people naturally liking you. One of the reasons you see yourself in a certain way is because of experiences that you've had in life. There is a way to use this idea to improve your performance and your enjoyment in your sport. After each game, review it to find your best plays, your best moves and anything positive. Get into the habit of remembering the positive things and you will build a positive image of yourself as an athlete. With this strong self-image you can then confidently look at your game to also find errors and identify the skills you want to further develop and the improvements you want to make.

This skill will help develop your 'recall' abilities which will naturally strengthen your concentration and focus. Another benefit is in your social life. Conversation is usually about remembering things that happen in our lives, so reviewing and talking about your game will also help you to be a better conversationalist. In career or profession, successful people often keep a log or a record of the activities to help them stay on track and plan for greater success. Learning to review your game now will make this valuable skill feel easy and natural in your future career as well as other areas of your life. *Imagine a future in which you know how to use your own experiences as lessons to bring you more success.*

Review your game to stay confident about your talent and skills, and to spot game errors. Remember, some of the very best lessons come from looking at your own performance.

~ Garo's Guidelines ~

*Some young athletes
learn a lot about life from their sport.*

*These young athletes
usually become very successful adults.*

Why not be one of them?

This book is like a piece of sports equipment.

*Just read a few chapters a week,
as long as you're in a sport.*

*The same way you condition physically
in your sport,
condition yourself for success and happiness
with this book.*

WHEN YOU USE THIS BOOK . . .

When you read a topic in this book, you are putting a idea in your mind that will make your life more positive and more fun. Here's how:

Every time you read a topic from this book, you are spending five minutes of your life in a very special way. The same way that practice and conditioning improves your sport, spending these five minutes only a few times a week will improve your enjoyment and success in life. You begin by choosing a topic that interests you at the moment. After you choose your topic, let's look at what you get in just a five-minute reading:

1) A statement that tells you the general importance of the positive trait.
2) The importance of the positive trait <u>in your sport</u>.
3) Tips and suggestions on developing the trait.
4) How the trait will benefit other areas of your life such as your school life, family life and friendships.
5) Although your career or profession may be years away, there are so many things you learn in your sport that will affect your work life. So we've included a brief positive idea to plant a seed in your mind.
6) Next, there's a statement *in italics* that begins with the word, 'Imagine'. The same way the career statement plants a seed for your work life, the *'Imagine'* statement plants a seed for your entire life.
7) Finally there's a statement encouraging you to remember the idea of the chapter.

Throughout this book, you'll see the word *success* mentioned often. Remember that true success is about things like: being yourself, reaching your own potential, having fun, and sharing good feelings with others. *Imagine a future in which you have a set of positive ideas that you can rely on to you bring success and happiness.* Keep up the good work and use this book regularly.

- Garo's Guidelines -

*Only when you
'feel' defeated
and let that feeling
bring you down in your sport*

then you've 'lost'.

*Learn from your performance
and keep that inner winning feeling
with you all the time
by giving steady effort
and staying confident
and optimistic.*

WHEN YOU LOSE A GAME . . .

When you lose a game . . . remember that the great athletes and teams learned the lessons *that made them great* from their losses. Here's how you can do the same:

After losing a game, look at the situation clearly. Start by looking at anything positive that you accomplished during the game. Then look at mistakes or errors so you can see exactly where you want to improve. If your team loses a lot, instead of focusing on winning, set smaller goals for improvement within the game. In other words, set goals that will allow you to win *the game of self-improvement.* Remember that the game is not first about winning, it's about playing. Look first to improve your playing and the wins will take care of themselves. If you are having bad feelings because of a loss, make those feelings count for something by learning from your loss. So many successful people in various fields point to the fact that their success came after numerous defeats.

Also realize that you are winning just by being in your sport. You can do this by looking at your real reasons for playing: being with your friends, the feeling of competing (being in the action), the actual nature of the game (enjoying the moves and the skills involved). It's about fun and learning.

This realization that it's all about fun and learning works in all areas of life. If you don't do well on a test, get back into the joy of learning and strive to learn more about the subject. Learn more about that person with whom you want to build a friendship. Learn more about your chores or part-time job and let the joy of learning and improving be your motivation to do them well. *Imagine a future where you are having fun and learning about life . . . and losses are simply used to get better at what you're doing.*

Remember whether you win or lose, enjoy 'the game', keep learning, and give your best effort.

- Garo's Guidelines -

*Little wins
lead up to
big wins.*

*To reach a big goal in your life,
go a little at a time
and stay determined.*

Let me spell that out for you

<u>G</u> <u>O</u> <u>A</u> <u>L</u>ittle
at a time

*and you will reach your goals
in your sport
and in your life.*

WHEN YOU SET GOALS...

When you set goals in your sport ... you begin a life of personal leadership. In other words, you begin to 'manage' your own life. Here's how it works:

As you play your sport, progress begins to happen naturally. Now if you want to be more in control of your progress, or if you want to *direct* your own progress or success, you can use something called goal-setting. Goals give you the opportunity to focus your effort in a very special way. This makes your achievement and progress as effective as possible. Goals also give you the feeling that you are always winning.

Using the power of goal-setting, you can choose a particular skill (or part of a skill) that you want to develop or improve, and concentrate your effort on that area. A goal allows you to score your effort by seeing whether you reach your goal within your set time-frame. So with a goal, you tend to put out more effort than when you don't have a goal. A goal moves you toward a particular target, so as you get closer to it you will keep up your effort, and even increase your effort as you start getting very close. In other words, goal-setting strengthens your determination. A goal can also make you very resourceful. When you commit yourself to a goal, you will figure out what it will take to reach it.

You can also use goal-setting in other areas of your life. Some important areas include: your education, family, friendships, leisure, health and fitness, work and earning money. In fact, if you have difficulty in any area of your life, look at the problem and set a goal and a specific time-frame to improve. *Imagine a life in which you are directing your own progress and managing your own success.*

Use goal-setting to improve yourself, but remember to keep the fun in your activities. Don't make your goals pressure you, make them positively challenge you.

- Garo's Guidelines -

*When you have
a star to follow,
there is always a light
to guide your path.*

*Always keep
a special dream goal
in your heart,
and its magic
will brighten your life.*

WHEN YOU SET LONG-RANGE GOALS . . .

When you set long-range goals in the development of your athletic skills . . . you are saying that you are truly serious about your sport. You are strengthening your sense of commitment. Let's look at this a little closer:

Once you've decided on a long-range commitment to your sport, discuss it with coaches and any other authorities who have followed young athletes' progress over a course of time. Let them evaluate you - your past performance and how you look now. Have them predict what can be expected of you in the time-frame that you are choosing to plan. Ask them what would be the least acceptable progress; a good or very good level of progress; and an outstanding or exceptional level of progress. Then have them help you to break that down into yearly or monthly performance goals.

Another benefit of having this type of long range commitment to your sport is that you begin to reduce or eliminate activities that can be personally wasteful or even destructive. You begin to develop positive qualities to support your athletic goals. For example, you'll naturally become more disciplined, cooperative, and self-aware because those are things required in your sport. Mentally, you'll find yourself more concentrated and you'll develop a mental toughness because these traits are obviously needed in your sport. Physically, you'll naturally become stronger and more resilient. So a sport is a very good place to set long-range goals. Remember in *any* area of life to look for guidance from people who have already reached the type of goals you are setting. This will be particularly helpful when you are ready to choose a career or profession. *Imagine a future in which you are always moving in a positive direction.*

Remember, once you set a long-range goal, stay focused and enjoy all the activities involved in reaching the goal.

~ Garo's Guidelines ~

*If I just gave you
$540
what would you do with it?*

*If you sleep 8 hours a day,
and you are in school 7 hours,
you have 9 hours
or 540 minutes left.*

*So everyday you have 540 valuable minutes
that are <u>yours</u> to use.*

*The way you use them will determine
the kind of person you will be . . .
so use them well!*

WHEN YOU MANAGE YOUR TIME . . .   32

When you manage your time to develop your skills and reach your goals . . . you are using a method that is used by the most successful people in the world. Here's more about the value of managing time:

Have you ever been on a vacation and been surprised at how much you've done in one day - how many things you've seen, how many places you visited, how many activities you fit into that one day. There's a lot that you can accomplish when you enjoy what you're doing. Managing your time is about planning your enjoyment in different segments throughout your day or your week

Your sport is a great place to learn time-management because goals are so clear - increase your strong performance and decrease your weak performance. This often translates to numbers - a lower numbers of errors, a greater number of catches, a lower number of misses, a greater number of hits, etc. Once you set your improvement goals, you can manage your activities within time-frames - an hour for this, fifteen minutes for that, and so on. The real fun happens when you have many different goals that all have their own time-frames. Managing more than one goal becomes important in other areas of life when you divide your time to enjoy various activities. Time for homework, time for play, some time on the phone, time for practice, etc. In career and professional life, adults agree that time-management is one of the most valuable and profitable skills you can have. *Imagine a future in which you have all the time you need to enjoy all the things you want.*

Remember that everything we do happens 'in time'. When you learn to manage all of your goals and activities, you are learning one of the very best ways to succeed in the game of life.

- Garo's Guidelines -

*There's a magical place
that you can go
to play your sport
and always
achieve your top performance.*

*This place is
your imagination.*

*Visit it often
and take its magic back
into your practice
and into your games.*

WHEN YOU IMAGINE A SUCCESSFUL PERFORMANCE..

When you imagine a successful performance and it happens . . . it feels like magic. Actually it is a natural ability that you have and can use to improve your skills in your sport and in your life. Here's how it works:

When you practice a skill, your body actually 'remembers' where your attention is being placed in your body. For example, if you throw a ball, attention is being placed on your hand, arm, shoulder and other parts of the body to different degrees. . . and this is what your body remembers. So if you perform a skill perfectly, your body has the memory to do it again and again. You just have to bring back that memory and let your body follow. If performance involves this kind of attention, it means that you can 'mentally' put your attention in those parts of the body and *'practice' by just imagining the skill in action.* The success of this has been proven repeatedly with all kinds of athletes from little league to world class teams.

You can start by watching a top athlete perform the skill you want to develop and then imagine yourself doing it in the same exact way. Then when you perform the skill you can practice remembering how it felt from start to finish. Actually feel the muscles and sense how your arms and legs are moving to create that perfect performance. When you hear people say that it's all about concentration, they are referring to this ability to concentrate your attention on making the right physical moves. In your everyday life you can practice this with any type of performance, such as making a presentation in front of your class. *Imagine any future that you want, and realize that what you 'imagine' can actually happen!*

Take a little time to imagine a successful performance in your sport and in other areas of your life, and watch how much easier your goals are reached.

~ Garo's Guidelines ~

*Congratulations
on where you are today!*

*Enjoy your feeling
of accomplishment.*

It took practice.

It took discipline.

You gave yourself to it.

You made it happen.

*You are successful
and you can be successful
in whatever you do.*

WHEN YOU'VE REACHED A NEW PERFORMANCE LEVEL... 34

When you've reached a new level of performance or reached a goal that you've been working toward... you are learning the meaning of success. Here's more about success:

You set a goal for yourself and now you've reached it. When reaching a goal, there are two things that athletes usually do. They look back at the work it took to reach the goal, and they look forward to their next goal. For some athletes, looking ahead can be a little stressful. Suddenly you realize that you *can* look forward, you *can* succeed. Whereas before you were just going along without feeling much pressure, now you may feel some pressure because you are *expected* to succeed. If you are feeling this, realize that you are feeling the same exact way that all the great athletes have felt at different points in their career. The answer is to congratulate yourself, and just settle into your new level of performance. Most importantly remember that you're in it because you enjoy it. Look at where you are now that you have reached this goal, and see what you are now enjoying about your new situation. Stay loose, relaxed and focused in your new activities.

Reaching goals is the meaning of success in all areas of life. In your schoolwork, you may have certain learning goals. You may have goals in your hobbies or in extracurricular activities. You may have a goal to have better relationships in your family and friendships. Reaching goals in your sport will prepare you to handle success in all these areas and more.
Imagine a future in which success is a natural and ongoing part of your life.

Remember when you reach a new level of performance, treat it as a personal victory, celebrate your victory, and then enjoy playing at your new level.

~ Garo's Guidelines ~

*Obstacles are really
what it's all about.*

*Without them,
we would have nothing
to test our strength,
our spirit
and our character.*

*Accept your obstacles,
and appreciate that
they are an important part
of the game of life.*

WHEN YOU HAVE AN OBSTACLE . . .   35

When you have an obstacle in your sport . . . you learn the valuable lesson that overcoming or removing obstacles is part of your 'inner game'. Let's take a closer look:

When you reach an obstacle, realize that you're progressing in your sport. The higher achievement that you see in successful athletes means that they went through those very same obstacles. So encountering an obstacle means that you are moving forward and you should see it in this positive way. See your obstacle as a way to get to a higher level of skill or a way of having more fun and satisfaction in your sport. In other words, translate your obstacle into an instruction. For example, the challenge you are feeling is actually telling you that you have to develop this skill or work a little harder in that particular area. Once you can do this, your athletic development will become more instinctive and you will move along at a much better personal pace. When you overcome or remove a large obstacle, congratulate yourself, reward yourself and look at how your life is different without that obstacle. Feel good about it, enjoy your new situation, and use your new confidence to work through other obstacles that may come up in your sport or your life.

This positive attitude toward obstacles will benefit you in all areas of life. In school life, your obstacles might be video games, TV, the phone or other things that stand between you and your homework. In making friends, your obstacle might be that it doesn't feel easy talking with people about yourself. Once you discover your obstacle you will know what you have to do, whether your goal involves your friendships, education or your family life. *Imagine a future in which everything (even your obstacles) contribute to your success.*

Remember whenever you are feeling unhappy, look for the obstacle that is causing it. Within the obstacle you're sure to find the solution.

− Garo's Guidelines −

*If obstacles
are good tests of strength,*

*then setbacks
are great tests of determination.*

*The greater
the challenge
you overcome,*

*the greater
the person
you become.*

*Setbacks are on
<u>every</u> path of greatness.*

WHEN YOU HAVE A SETBACK...

When you have a setback and recover from it... you are following the course of all the truly great athletes. Here's more about it:

Recovering from a setback means experiencing some kind of 'failure' and coming back a winner. The great athletes are the ones who have suffered great defeat and lifted themselves up to great victory. If you have a setback that makes it longer than you expected to reach a goal, remember that your sport is first about the enjoyment of playing the game and second about the results. Look at the area of your setback, get totally involved in that area and bring out the satisfaction and fun. This is one of the most constructive ways to handle a setback - to turn the negative into a positive, to keep everything upbeat and to develop the character and strength that will make you a durable athlete. Realize that people who don't run into setbacks along the way may have a great disappointment later on when they encounter a big challenge that they haven't built up enough resilience and 'comeback' power to handle.

So understand that setbacks are part of the big picture in your sport. With this outlook, you'll be able to handle them when they occur. Remembering that you're in the game for the long run will help you to put setbacks into their proper perspective.

Getting back on track after a setback is one of the best ways to prepare for challenges in life. When you've encountered enough setbacks, you realize that you need *to be ready* for them. In life, this will help you to better prepare for special challenges in your career, profession, finances, relationships and other areas. *Imagine a future in which you have that extra strength and resilience to handle any kind of setback.*

Remember that each setback that you encounter is a great opportunity to build your strength and your toughness.

− Garo's Guidelines −

Feeling stressed?

*Here is an
<u>instant</u> solution.*

*Just stop focusing on what you're feeling
and start focusing on
what you're 'doing'.*

*You won't feel a harmful kind of stress
when you're
totally involved in what you're doing.*

*You can see your challenges
as a way to failure
or a way to success.*

*The way you <u>see</u> them
is what they will bring to your life.*

WHEN YOU FEEL STRESSED . . .

When you feel stressed . . . you are *choosing* to feel that way. Let's look at another choice you can make:

When something happens that is very challenging, some people get stressed by it. They become unhappy, they get worried, their performance drops. If it's really bad, they can lose their appetite, lose sleep and even feel sick about it. These people take a challenge and turn it into stress. Other people will look at the same challenges and see them as opportunities to get tough and move closer to their goals. If life didn't have challenges, there would be no sense of accomplishment or feeling of achievement. So first realize that challenges are good, and that it's a person's reaction to challenges that can make them seem bad. There is something to learn and something to gain from every single challenge you encounter in your sport, whether it's about developing your skills, handling defeat, working with other people, etc. Your sport is one of the best places to learn how to see challenges in this more positive way. Once you begin getting stronger, you will actually begin to look for those harder challenges to test your toughness. If at any time you are feeling stressed (or too stressed), talk to your coach, your parents or another trusted person.

Seeing challenges in a positive way is a success trait that will naturally help you in all areas of your life. School life, friendships and especially family life all have challenges that you can use to strengthen yourself (and others involved).
Imagine a future in which you are calmly and effectively handling the challenges of life.

Remember that 'stress' is a choice. If you feel stressed, you are taking a situation in your life and making it affect you in a harmful way. Instead, look for *the challenge* in the situation and find a way to meet the challenge - a way that works for your *personally*.

~ Garo's Guidelines ~

*If the world is beginning to look dark
remember that there is a light
that the right people in your life
can show you how to see.*

*If the world is beginning to feel too crowded
remember that there is a clearing
that the right people in your life
can show you how to find.*

*If you ever feel like quitting
<u>anything</u>,
share your feelings
with the important people in your life.*

It <u>will</u> help.

WHEN YOU FEEL LIKE QUITTING . . .

When you feel like quitting . . . you have one of the best opportunities to learn about problem-solving and decision - making. Here's why:

If you want to leave your sport so that you can do something else with your time, or to play a different sport, you are <u>not</u> quitting. You're just redirecting your life, and it's something you'll do often throughout your life. <u>If you want to quit to escape problems</u>, realize that the types of problems that you're trying to escape may show up in other areas of your life. So your real choice is whether you want to handle them now or handle them later. The biggest problem with handling them later is that when you run from problems, your fear of them gets greater the next time you encounter them. So, let's say you've decided to deal with them now. What do you do next? First, consider that your basic problem is not about your sport at all. It's really about your ability to manage different goals. So begin by turning your problems into goals. For example, turn 'a problem with my coach' into the goal of 'having a better relationship with my coach'. After you turn all of your problems into goals, take a look at them and determine which is the most important or which one you want to work on first.

You can do this with every area of your life. In your school life, your friendships, your family life, there will always be problems or challenges. By learning to see your problems as goals, you're learning how to win the inner game. In career or professional life, the most successful people are naturally the ones who see problems in this constructive way. *Imagine a future in which you can turn all problems into goals and then enjoy reaching your goals.*

Keep up the good work, my friend. When you have a lot of problems, remember to turn them into goals and handle the most important ones first . . . and don't forget you can always ask for help.

~ Garo's Guidelines ~

*The best way
to become a leader
is to first be a follower.*

*In other words,
when you follow someone's instructions,
it makes it easier for you
to have people follow your instructions.*

*A great place to start
is with that special person
who helps you to get
the most out of your sport -*

your coach!

WHEN YOU FOLLOW YOUR COACH'S INSTRUCTIONS . . .

When you follow your coach's instructions . . . you are learning an essential personal leadership skill. Here's why this sports experience is so important:

Your coach is in a leadership role in your sport. It is his role to teach you and to guide you in your athletic development and in some areas of your personal and social development. By learning to follow instructions given by your coach, you are accepting his or her authority. This quality will make it easier for you to accept yourself as a leader in other areas of your life and in your future, because you will see leadership as a positive quality. See the positive results that can come from your coach's instruction and the improvement in your athletic skill, but focus on *the enjoyment and the involvement of learning* more than the result. In this way, the results will come about in the best possible way. Recognize when you have developed the new skill and look for further instructions.

Bring your ability and willingness to follow instructions into other areas of your life and you'll see great results. If your doctor gives you instructions, you follow them because you know that it will make you well. Realize that listening to your teachers will result in your educational well-being and listening to your parents will contribute to the well-being of your family life. In your future career or profession, the better you can follow instructions, the higher will be your income, your satisfaction in your work and your influence. Learning to follow instructions and guiding others to follow instructions is the basis of a successful future. *Imagine a future in which you can confidently learn skills that are required in your work life or desired in your personal life.*

Remember that when you follow your coach's instructions, you're not only learning the athletic skill, but you are also learning how to follow instructions in general, which is a trait that will help you throughout your life.

~ Garo's Guidelines ~

*By <u>allowing</u> your coach to correct you,
you allow yourself to get
stronger and better.*

*By <u>accepting</u> your coach's corrections,
you are accepting the way to success
into your life.*

*By <u>wanting</u> your coach to correct you,
you are personally deciding
to succeed in your life.*

*By <u>looking forward to</u> your coach's corrections,
you are playing the inner game
and you <u>will</u> succeed in your life.*

WHEN YOU ARE CORRECTED BY YOUR COACH...

When you are corrected by your coach . . . you are saving all that time that it would take you to correct your mistake on your own. Here's more on the value of having someone you can count on to correct your mistakes:

If your coach realizes that you know how to correct your own mistake, they'll just point it out and they won't give you a lesson on it. If they think you don't know how to handle the problem, they'll give you instruction. Your coach might first compliment you on something you do well, give you the correction, then finally assure you that you'll do well in correcting your mistake and improving your skill.

If you break a team rule and your coach uses a form of corrective punishment, realize the feeling is that you and the coach together are attacking the problem and that the coach is not ever attacking you personally. Look at it as a learning experience and don't make yourself feel bad about it. Simply take responsibility for the fact that the rule has been broken. Realize the penalty, accept it, and appreciate that the penalty is aimed at the problem and not at you personally.

There are people who have gone through the steps that you are now taking in different areas of your life. These people can help you when you make a mistake. Why not use their experience to solve your problem? You can rely on parents, teachers, counselors, relatives, friends and others. When you learn through correction it means that you are very 'coachable' . . . and coachable people who can follow successful people become successful themselves. *Imagine a future in which you are helped by successful people to become successful in your own life.*

Keep up the good work, my friend. When you are corrected, see it in terms of how it will help you to improve. Want it, take it and use it for your success!

~ Garo's Guidelines ~

Feelings affect your thoughts.

Thoughts affect your performance.

Your performance affects your results.

Your results affect your feelings.

Your feelings affect your thoughts.

Your thoughts affect your performance.

And on it goes.

*Everything is affected
by how you feel.*

*Work on sharing your feelings,
and good things will follow.*

WHEN YOU SHARE FEELINGS WITH YOUR COACH...

When you share your feelings with your coach... you are using a unique way to unlock your potential. Here's why sharing your feelings is such a good idea:

All the great athletes will tell you that great performance begins with *how you feel*. If you feel great, you play great, and if you feel unhappy or stressed, it will probably show in your performance. So if you are having bad feelings about something, the best thing to do is get in touch with them and resolve them so they won't affect your playing. Sometimes it's hard to share feelings with people, mainly because bad feelings often occur because of something that happened with people. But your coach is a very special person. His (or her) purpose is to help you reach your best sports performance. So if helping you work through your feelings will get you to your best performance, then you can see that sharing your feelings *is part of your athletic development*. Realize that your coach knows that it is important to understand what you are thinking and feeling.

A survey of young people showed that the easiest thing for them to share with their parents was their sports involvement and the hardest thing was how they felt about themselves. So your sport may just be the place to begin sharing your feelings because of their effect on your sports performance. Then you can more easily open up to your parents, teachers and friends. In your future career or profession, your personal individual feelings will often hold the key to success. *Imagine a future in which you are free of emotional problems and feel good about yourself and about life every day.*

Remember that emotion is a powerful force. When you get in touch with your feelings by sharing them with your coach, you can more easily use this force to give your best performance and experience success and happiness.

~ Garo's Guidelines ~

*Now is the time
to accept one of the easiest
ways to succeed.*

*Learn from people
who are succeeding.*

*Now is the time
to accept one of the easiest
ways to be happy.*

*Learn from people
who are happy.*

*Start by asking athletes
who are a little older than you
for some tips or suggestions
on how to get better.*

WHEN YOU ARE COACHED BY OLDER PLAYERS...

When you are coached by older players . . . you are taking a reliable and natural path toward success. Here's why:

In your sport, there is a natural progression of learning. You start with the fundamentals in practice, then you begin making good plays in games, and after a while your athletic performance begins to feel natural. Since every young athlete in your sport goes through the same progression, a great way to learn is to get advice or be coached by an older or more experienced player. The benefit is that the older player is just enough ahead of your own development to still be interested in talking about it. In other words, it would also help them to be able to talk about how they developed their skill or reached their goal. Talking about the skill helps them to review it and prepares them for their next goal.

In family life, you can learn from an older brother or sister how to do certain things or how to avoid certain mistakes. You can even ask your parents what they did at your age. This will also help you and your parents to understand each other. In school life, you can look to students in higher grades for guidance. Most of us have friends of different ages, so your friendships are a great place to learn from people who are a little older than you. In career and professional life, it is a fact of life that new people learn from the people who are more experienced in the company or organization. Taking the initiative now to learn from more experienced people in your sport will prepare you for this important part of life. *Imagine a future in which you learn from the people who have achieved the same exact goals you are striving to achieve.*

Remember that one of the easiest and fun ways to succeed in a particular area is to learn from people who have already succeeded in that area.

- Garo's Guidelines -

*What do you think happens
when you learn something,
and then help someone else to learn it?*

*You feel good about yourself.
The person you coached feels good about you.
You feel good about them.
People who know you feel good about you.
You then also feel good about them.*

A lot of good feelings!

*And you can do this by sharing
anything you know
with anyone who needs it.*

*By giving a little of your thoughts,
you'll get back a lot of good feelings.*

WHEN YOU COACH SOMEONE...

When you coach someone . . . you are learning valuable leadership traits that will bring you success in all areas of your life. Here's more about it:

In your sport, you may be given the opportunity to coach someone or be an assistant coach. In your coaching role, you would be helping young athletes to: develop skills, to work and play well with others, to keep the fun in your sport, to help them succeed in their individual positions and as part of the team, and finally to develop those inner traits and qualities that will serve them well both in their sport and in their life.

There are two basic coaching styles. One way is to try to make someone perform well so that they'll avoid punishment. The other way is to encourage people to do well so they experience all the positive rewards of good performance. The punishment style of coaching can produce: anxiety and worry in your athletes, less enjoyment, incidents of lateness and skipping practices, quitting, bad relationships with the coach and other people on the team. This style creates the feeling of being wrong and tends to make the player feel bad about himself. In the positive style, the coach focuses more on complimenting the little successes along the way, rather than focusing on the mistakes. With this kind of coaching, young athletes tend to want to come to practice and to stay in their sport. They feel better about themselves, and they can relate more easily to their coach and other people on the team.

By coaching someone in your sport, you are preparing for leadership in other areas of your life. These same basic principles of leadership also apply to every career and profession. *Imagine a future in which you are prepared to be a leader when the situation calls for it.*

When you help someone else to learn something, you are also learning something very valuable - how to be a leader.

~ Garo's Guidelines ~

*If you had a dream
in which you were
playing a championship game
and made all the right moves,
(and you had the same dream every night)
do you think that the dream would somehow
help you to get better in real life
and become a champion?*

*Sometimes we take TV for granted.
It's like a 'dream screen'
where we can see visions of anything we want
and use them to motivate us.*

*Create your own dream goals
and use 'the dream screen'
to help you to make them happen
in real life.*

WHEN YOU USE TV TO LEARN ABOUT YOUR SPORT...

When you use TV to learn about your sport . . . you are preparing for your future in a very special way. Here's more about it:

Wouldn't it be great to have a tool with which you could see the best athletes in the world perform, and then replay their performance to watch every detail of their best moves? We have such a tool, but we use it so much for entertainment, many of us think that entertainment is its only use. This amazing tool is TV. The pros know the value of watching video-taped games, and do it all the time. How can you use the TV to improve your own playing? One way is to watch a game and focus on the position that you play. If you tape the game, you have an added benefit. When the player who has your position makes the play, replay it a few times until you can sense every physical movement that the athlete made throughout the entire play. So instead of seeing one thing (the play) you might be seeing ten of more activities that make up the play. By seeing the breakdown of movements, you can see both the order of the movements and the player's physical coordination (for example, how the movements of the arms and legs coordinate to make a smooth performance). This will guide your performance.

A way to use TV constructively in other areas of life is to look for programs about things that genuinely interest you. Ask your parents to watch a show with you and then ask what they thought of it. This will help you to watch more actively and develop your concentration. In your future, screen learning and communication will be very important. *Imagine a future in which you feel comfortable using the newest and best methods of learning and communications.*

Keep up the good work. Set aside some time every week to use TV, video or computer for <u>learning</u>.

~ Garo's Guidelines ~

You can learn from books.
A book is a collection of ideas
written by someone who learned ideas
from their experience of life.

You can learn from people.
People will teach you what they have learned
through their experience of life.

Whose experience of life
do you think will teach you
the very best lessons?

Your own!

Take a little time every week
to see what you're learning from your own
experiences in your sport and your life.

WHEN YOU LEARN 'FROM YOURSELF'...

When you learn 'from yourself'... you are discovering your personal talents and bringing them out naturally. Let's look at exactly how you learn 'from yourself':

What does it mean to learn 'from yourself'? A good way to understand this is to imagine the very first people who played your sport. In a way, the sport was really something they learned 'from themselves' since no one else had invented it yet. So it just came out of the pure fun they were having. When you get in touch with <u>your own personal</u> fun you're having, you are doing what those very first athletes did - you are discovering your sport for yourself and learning as you go along by simply watching your own development. Then you'll naturally want to start improving your moves so you can have even more fun. Practice won't *feel* like practice, it will just feel like fun. The way your arms, hands and legs move, the way your mind reacts, the way your eyes focus, and the way your personal feelings affect your playing are all the things that make you 'who you are' in your sport - that make you unique. These are very valuable things that you just can't learn from anyone other than yourself. Start becoming aware of all these things about 'you'. Learn from yourself how to get the best from yourself.

You can also learn 'from yourself' in other areas of life. Learn from yourself your own natural way that you talk and express yourself. Learn from yourself the kind of friend you are. Decide your own personal best way to learn in school and to contribute in your family life. Keep in mind that the greatest success in life belongs to the person who can learn from his or her own experience. *Imagine a future in which your success naturally comes out of who you are as a person.*

Remember to learn from your own experiences, your own talents, and to listen to your heart. You will find that in a lot of ways, *you* can be your own best teacher.

- Garo's Guidelines -

*Follow the career
of a professional athlete*

*and you'll learn that
being a professional,
being a champion,
being the best
happens:*

*one
step
at
a
time*

*Keep making those steady
small improvements every week
and the big rewards <u>will</u> come.*

WHEN YOU FOLLOW A TEAM OR A PLAYER . . .

When you follow a team or a player . . . you are learning the value of a role model. Let's take a look what it means to have a positive role model:

A professional (or college) athlete who plays your position can be a powerful role model. But what does it really mean to have a role model? Well there are two sides of yourself - your *real self* and your *role self*. Your role self is the 'you' that acts a part, whether the part is the position you play in your sport, your academic role as a student or your family role (the way you contribute in your home life). If you have a part-time job or do community service, you are serving in a role. When you do well in a role, you also strengthen your real self. Your real self is the 'you' that reflects on how you feel about life. Things like happiness, confidence, enthusiasm, satisfaction, empowerment are all felt by your real self, but are often reached through the activities in your roles. Since you are participating in a role in your sport, why not look for someone who has done well in that role and model your performance, your attitude and habits after that person. This is the true meaning of having a role model.

Role modeling can be used effectively in other areas of life. If there is someone you admire, whether it's a parent, a teacher or a friend, you might want to get to know them better to learn how they developed the positive traits that you admire. In your future career or profession, learning about the leaders in your field or the organization you're working for will help to assure your growth and advancement. *Imagine a future filled with examples of success that you can follow to reach your own success.*

When you have a goal, look for people who have already reached that goal or a similar goal, and follow their example of positive traits, skills, habits and attitude.

~ Garo's Guidelines ~

Everything that gets done,

*gets done
by people,
for people,
with people,
through people.*

Our world is about people.

<u>*Your*</u> *world is about people.*

*Develop your ability
to listen attentively
and to learn from what you're hearing,*

*and you'll see just how valuable
people are in your life.*

WHEN YOU LEARN ABOUT YOUR SPORT FROM PEOPLE . . .   47

When you learn about your sport from people . . . you are also learning *about people*. Let's look at the value of listening to people who are 'talking sports'.

People like to talk sports. In listening to people talk sports, you are going to hear people who have different *types* of knowledge and different *amounts* of knowledge. A parent, a cousin, a neighbor or one of your adult relatives may know certain things and have certain opinions. Teammates, older players, assistant coaches and coaches may have different ideas. Professional players and sports authorities that you see on TV will have yet another level of knowledge. When listening to anyone talk about your sport, learn to evaluate what you are hearing. To determine the value of what you're learning, ask yourself if what you are learning is helping you to enjoy your sport or improve your performance.

This idea is important in all areas of life, because so much of what we learn in life comes directly form other people. First you learn from your parents, relatives and neighbors. Then you go to school and learn from teachers. Then you join a sport and learn from your coach. Through it all, you are also learning about life from your friends, cousins, classmates, teammates and others who are your age. Whenever you listen to people talking about something that's important to you (such as your schoolwork, part-time job or a personal interest or past time), listen for what will help you to enjoy that area of your life or help to improve your performance. Naturally, this quality will be most important in your future career or profession. *Imagine a future in which people in all areas of your life help you to meet your challenges and reach goals.*

Remember that your world is made up of people. When you learn to listen carefully, people in all areas of your life can guide you to success and happiness.

~ Garo's Guidelines ~

*The most important things
that happen in life,*

the most important ideas,

the most valuable knowledge,

the greatest secrets to success,

all the best stuff

*always
winds up in a
book.*

*Don't think of a book as
something you <u>have to</u> read.*

*Think of a book as a way
to find out things you <u>want to</u> know.*

WHEN YOU READ ABOUT YOUR SPORT . . .

When you read about your sport . . . it can be one of the most fun and easy ways to keep the excitement alive in your sport. Here's why:

You have 'roles' in life. You are a student, a friend, a helper in your house. You may be a member of a club or an actor in a school play. When you join a sport, you chose to take on a very special role - the role of an athlete. Just like an actor's role, your athletic role also means that you are playing a part. The part you play as an athlete has been played by many people in the past. By reading about these people you can learn what it means to be a great athlete. When you read a book about a particular star athlete, look for their character traits that made them great. What about them shows their confidence, their energy, their toughness? See where you can bring these traits into your own life. When you find these traits that you admire, make them part of your personality.

You might want to also read general information books about your sport. It might be fun to read about the terms and words used in your sport, the players and equipment, the field or playing area, the skills required, how the game is played. You might also like learning how leagues are arranged, the early development of the sport, how it spread in popularity, what it looks like today. When you think about it, reading is the most important skill in today's world for someone who wants to achieve success. Naturally, the successful people in career and professional life are those who can learn information and use it effectively. *Imagine a future in which the world of knowledge is open to you because of your love of reading and learning.*

Keep up the good work. Remember, reading is an important fact of life. The more that you enjoy reading and learning, the more success and happiness you'll find in life.

~ Garo's Guidelines ~

*No matter what anyone says,
how any one acts,
how anyone thinks or feels
about your sport,
never believe
that your sport is meant to be stressful.*

*It's meant to be fun
The harder you play,
the more fun you'll have.*

*We say
'Play the sport.'
not
'Work the sport.'*

*Be a player,
and if you want the best fun
you can possibly imagine,
be the best player you can be.*

WHEN YOU 'PLAY HARD' AT YOUR SPORT...

When you play hard at your sport . . . you are giving everything you've got. Let's take a look at what it means to play hard at your sport:

How do you feel when you change the phrase 'hard work' to 'hard fun'. It gives it a whole different feeling, doesn't it? That's what a sport is - hard fun. Working hard at your sport is actually *playing* hard. It's what happens when you give yourself to it - when you cross that line and say, "I'm here, I'm in it, I'm not backing off. I'll do whatever it takes to have <u>all</u> the fun." Always keep in mind that a sport is about learning and fun. You're not in a real war, you're not in a real battle. There is not real danger. But there is the spirit and the feeling of competition . . . and that's part of what makes it fun.

Also realize there is a difference between play and pleasure. Play is something that requires real skill. Pleasure is a good feeling that you don't need a particular skill to experience. For example, watching TV and just being entertained without really participating can give you pleasure. Too much pleasure can be destructive. Play is constructive. Play hard in your sport and you'll be preparing to enjoy life much more than if you just look for pleasure.

When you bring the spirit of hard play into other areas, you'll create a complete change in the way you live, work and relate to others.. Even in the business world, the truly successful ones are called 'players', because they are the ones who are personally <u>choosing</u> their work, and therefore playing the game of business. The key is to play hard and give it everything you've got. *Imagine a future where you are playing hard and totally enjoying the game of life.*

Remember when you *think* the words, 'hard <u>work</u>', *feel* the words, 'hard <u>play</u>'.

~ Garo's Guidelines ~

*Being in the moment
gives you a very special advantage.*

*It allows you
to instantly forget a mistake
and to move on.*

*This is the secret of the great athletes
who win at the buzzer
or who break a tie
in the final moments of a game.*

*Learn from your mistakes,
but go on
and stay focused
on each passing moment of your playing.*

WHEN YOU ARE 'IN THE MOMENT'...

When you play your sport and you are in the moment, totally involved and completely focused . . . you are reaching the highest level of performance that any athlete can attain. So let's talk about this great feeling a little bit:

'In the moment' is the place where athletes can find perfection. Being 'in the moment' is one of the greatest feelings in the world. This comes from keeping up your fundamentals to the point where you don't have to think about them in play. As soon as you experience this great feeling, your motivation to practice will increase considerably. Until you reach that experience, have faith that there is that magical feeling and that it is possible for you to achieve it. Watching the greats at a game or on TV will help you to realize what they are feeling when they are 'in the zone'. Going over great plays on video tape, rewinding and rewatching them is also a good way to see what it means to be at this level of performance.

A word about winning: Although the outcome of the game is important, it can take an athlete 'out of the moment'. The desire to win can become a distraction if your mind wanders away from your total focus and involvement in the game to worrying about whether you're going to win. Give yourself to the game. This is where you'll find your enjoyment - your fun - and that's the first and most important reason to play. Naturally, when you bring the feeling of total involvement into your schoolwork, family and friendships, you become more attentive, and you find people becoming more attentive to you and your thoughts and feelings. *Imagine a future of total involvement in all the things that you love to do . . . and with the people who are most important to you.*

You've worked hard to prepare. Now just 'let yourself go' . . . and be 'in the moment' in your sport. Do this throughout your life and you'll have more enjoyment and success in life.

~ Garo's Guidelines ~

*If you don't care about being great,
okay, then maybe you'll be good.*

*If you don't care about being good,
okay, then maybe you'll be average.*

*If you don't care about being average,
okay, then maybe you'll be below-average.*

*But as long as you're playing,
you will be <u>something</u>.*

Why not expect that you'll be great?

*Then look realistically at where you are,
and do what it takes to become great -
one step at a time.*

WHEN YOU EXPECT THE BEST FROM YOURSELF . . .

When you expect the best from yourself . . . you are setting a course for success with one of the most positive traits you can have. Here's how the power of positive expectancy works:

To expect the best from yourself, you first have to have that strong belief that you can actually bring out your best. This belief comes from being mentally and physically well-prepared and from having the right feelings about what you are doing.

To get into the habit of expecting the best from yourself, you first have to be clear on what it means to be at your very best. This means being realistic about where you are in your skills and having an idea of what would happen if you played at the top of your talent and skill. Ask your coach to evaluate your skills and give you some goals that will represent your potential with the skills you have. If you believe your coach and you have confidence in yourself, then you can expect this level of performance from yourself. You can also look at other players who are higher than you in their skills and begin to expect yourself to play at their level.

Expect your personal best in your school work. Expect yourself to be the best son, daughter, brother or sister you can be. Who is your best friend? What makes you such a good friend *to them*? Throughout your life you will see that *being* your best at anything always begins with *expecting* your best. *Imagine a future in which you can count on your best to bring you success and happiness.*

Remember that expecting the best from yourself blocks out distractions and allows you to focus on your own 'inner game' of personal development. That's why expecting the best from yourself is a direct path to success in your sport and in other important areas of your life.

~ Garo's Guidelines ~

*Don't make 'good habits'
into something
difficult and unnatural.*

*The moon keeps going around the earth,
the earth keeps going around the sun,
the waves keep crashing on the shore.*

*Are they practicing good habits
or are they doing
what is natural for them to do?*

*See how what you're doing
is natural for your success,
natural for your enjoyment,
and natural for <u>you</u>*

*and you'll just want to keep doing them . . .
. . . naturally!*

WHEN YOU WORK ON A GOOD HABIT ... 52

When you work on developing a good habit ... you are learning the easiest way to assure happiness and success in life. Here's more about the power of good habits:

When you begin to develop a good habit, it might feel uncomfortable because it's new and you have to take a little time and effort to make it a part of your day (or week). After you do it for a while, it begins to feel familiar. After you do it enough times, it begins to feel natural. Some people believe that after you repeat a habit every day for twenty-one days, you can then fully accept it into your life.

When you develop a new skill in your sport, you are forming a habit. The more you work at it, the more natural it feels. If the skill helps you to reach your goals, you call it a positive or 'good' habit. Your sport is a place where many good habits are formed, not only in athletic skills but also in working and playing with others and developing a positive attitude. An *attitude* is a habit of how you think and feel. In your sport, you learn to focus and concentrate your *thoughts* and to bring out the right *feelings* to play your best, so your sport is a great place to develop a strong positive attitude.

Since you have goals in all areas of your life, learning to develop positive habits is a valuable quality. When you do a little to help around the house *every day*, soon it no longer feels like a chore. It just feels natural. Doing your homework consistently and having regular ongoing friendships are great examples of the value of good habits. *Imagine a future in which you can rely on the power of developing positive habits to be successful and happy.*

Remember there is one absolute thing you can count on in life. When you do something over and over, it eventually feels natural and easy to do. So if there is <u>anything</u> you want to accomplish or change in your life, remember that <u>you have the power to do it by forming the right habits</u>.

~ Garo's Guidelines ~

*How would you act
if you were in a
professional world championship game?*

*Think about it
and see what happens
when you act that way
in your everyday practices and games.*

*Act with a positive sense of pride
that comes from your gratefulness
for the gifts you've been given.*

*Do the same in the game of life
and you're sure to be a winner.*

WHEN YOU HAVE POSITIVE PRIDE...

When you have positive pride . . . you are confidently aware of your positive traits, skills and talents. Here's more about this special quality:

There is only one of you in the entire world. You are unique, with your own special talents, skills, and strengths. These are reasons to be proud of yourself. The pride that we're talking about isn't selfish. It simply says you are aware that you are using the gifts you have been given. In playing a sport, you are also deciding to express certain positive traits. When you have a healthy pride in yourself, you want to develop and show the most positive traits, because you will be known for them. For example, you would want to be known as a person who has courage, who works hard, who is humble in victory and gracious in defeat, who gives himself totally to the game, who is well-mannered and plays by the rules, who is optimistic. To develop positive pride, think of the type of person you feel deserves to be recognized and admired, then plan what you have to do to become that person. Look at yourself thoughtfully. See both your good points and those areas that you want to improve. Sharpen your good points and strive to improve your weaker areas.

The best kind of pride is the one that recognizes that your gifts come from a Higher Being. This is evident in those fine athletes who, after a great play or a goal, make a gesture that points to their belief in this Higher Being. Bring your pride into other areas of your life. Be proud of the fact that you're a good friend. Be proud that you're a good son, daughter, brother or sister. In a part-time job or a career, positive pride assures your coworkers that your work will be done with pride. *Imagine a future in which you can depend on your positive pride to bring you success and happiness.*

Keep up the good work. Remember, with positive pride you are presenting yourself to the world as a successful person.

~ Garo's Guidelines ~

To take up the habit of success
you have to give up any habits that
(in any way)
can block you, weaken you,
or slow down your pace.

Bad habits can be sneaky.

Without you knowing
exactly how it happened,
one really bad habit
can gradually take away
all that you've accomplished!

Be watchful.

If you have bad habits,
reduce or remove them from your life
one-day-at-a-time.

WHEN YOU WORK ON REMOVING A BAD HABIT... 54

When you work on removing a bad habit . . . you're taking control of your life in a very special way. Here's more about it:

Few people have personal trainers who watch them perform everyday, correcting them and showing them where to adjust their performance. Most of us learn the basics from coaches, and most of the time we learn on our own. When we're on our own and we're not sure of a precise way to handle a situation, we might create our own solutions. Many times our solutions work. Sometimes they work, but they don't work as well as they should. That's when we might develop a bad habit and keep building the habit until we're shown a better way. That's why it's important to regularly ask your coach to look at your performance and to advise you where to adjust.

In other areas of life we might choose solutions that give us quick answers, but go against us in the long run. Obviously using drugs, tobacco or alcohol are bad habits that can do us actual physical harm. Then there are the more common bad habits, like watching homework with the TV on, staying up too late, using bad language (because we don't know what else to say to feel 'cool'). To remove bad habits from your life, watch the things you do. When you spot a bad habit, you might want to first work on *reducing* it. Do a little less each week until it's no longer a part of your life. In your future career or profession, the ability to spot any bad habits and correct them before they grow too big will be very important. *Imagine a future in which you have the strength and character to remove any bad habits that are blocking you from true success and happiness.*

Learn to spot bad habits before they get too big by watching for anything you do in your sport or your life that could be weakening you, preventing you from moving forward, or blocking you from reaching your goals.

~ Garo's Guidelines ~

The Athlete's
Energy Food - Shopping List

Fruit,
Vegetables (especially green, leafy veggies),
Salads,
Whole grain breads, Cereals, Pasta,
Turkey, Chicken,
Meats (grilled or broiled),
'No yolk' egg substitutes (or egg whites),
Yogurt,
Fruit Juice.

Tip: Substitute fruit juice sweetened jelly
for sugar wherever you can.
(for example, to sweeten plain yogurt)

Suggest to your family
to add or have more of these
in your menu,
and you'll add and have more energy
in your sport and in your life.

WHEN YOU EAT THE RIGHT FOODS . . .

When you eat the right foods and have good nutritional habits . . . you are giving your body what it needs *so that it can give you what you want* **- energy for your best performance, and health for a happy life. Here's more:**

A lot of the enjoyment in your sport comes from the energy you put into your athletic performance. An essential source of your energy comes from the foods you eat. So one reason to eat right is that it will put more power and fun into your sport. There are many general benefits of eating right. By avoiding the wrong foods, you don't physically stress your body so it allows you to *relax* more easily. The right nutrition lets you pull all the energy from the food you are eating so you can *exercise* more easily. When you form the habit of eating right you tend to continue the good habit and your energy will continue to increase.

Nutrition is about everything that you put into your body. In this regard, what you eat is one of the most personal choices that you make in life -- choosing what's actually becoming a physical part of your body.

You shouldn't feel pressured into eating the right foods. One way to not feel pressured is to actually help design your family's meals. Look at what's in the refrigerator or on the shelves and suggest things that you would like to try. If there is something you don't like but know you should be eating, start by eating just a little, and you'll begin developing a taste for it. *Imagine a future in which you always feel mentally, physically and emotionally strong because you can count on your nutrition to provide you with the energy that you need.*

Keep up the good work, and treat your body right with good nutrition. In return, your body will give you its maximum performance in your sport and in your life.

~ Garo's Guidelines ~

*There are things you can get in life
by being lucky.*

Physical fitness is not one of them.

*To be healthy and strong,
you must earn it
by exercising and conditioning.*

*Make the choice today to exercise.
When tomorrow comes,
make the choice again.*

*Claim your body for your own,
and give it what you know it wants -
good physical exercise.*

*Set aside time every day,
and have fun in your
exercise and conditioning program!*

WHEN YOU EXERCISE AND CONDITION . . .

When you exercise and condition . . . you are giving yourself an edge that you can bring into your sport and into all areas of your life. Here's more about it:

Exercise is activity that causes you to breathe a little more heavily. Exercise comes in many different forms such as: running, jogging, playing tennis, throwing a Frisbee, riding a bike, swimming, fast walking, and naturally, playing your sport.

Whenever you exercise or condition vigorously, your body releases natural chemicals that relax you. You'll notice that after a good workout your body has that relaxed feeling. In this way, exercise helps to relieve stress. More exercise gives you more energy and the more energy you have, the more you want to exercise. So exercise will make you stronger and stronger. Exercise also naturally burns calories, brings up your metabolism and lowers your appetite, so it also helps you to maintain very good nutritional habits. Conditioning helps to build your endurance so you won't get tired in the later stages of your games. Having more stamina from good exercise and conditioning can give you an edge with players who have other types of advantages over you.

Realize that exercise and conditioning is not just for the season, but should be a regular year-round activity. To build endurance, strive to continually improve your repetitions, your distance or your time, so that you form a habit of growth - that is, a habit of surpassing your previous limits. *Imagine a future in which you always feel mentally, physically and emotionally strong because you can count on your excellent exercise habits to provide you with the energy that you need.*

Remember that the quality of your work improves and the enjoyment of your activities is greater when you're in good physical shape.

- Garo's Guidelines -

*You can have
all the right thoughts
and all the right feelings,*

*but if you don't have
the physical energy,*

*you won't be able to
make the moves to reach your goals
in your sport and in your life.*

*One of nature's best ways
to restore and build your energy
is sleep.*

*The deeper and more restful your sleep,
the more energy you will have the next day.*

Sleep well.

WHEN YOU GET A GOOD NIGHT'S SLEEP ...

When you get a good night's sleep . . . your body completely rejuvenates itself and prepares you to perform at your very best in whatever you do. Let's look a little further into the value of a good night's sleep:

All the natural traits and qualities that you most need in your sport are greatly increased after a good night's sleep. After deep sleep, your energy is restored, you become calm and even-tempered, your concentration is fully renewed, your thinking is very clear and your senses are strengthened. This happens due to the slowing down of your breathing and heart rate, and the rejuvenation that occurs in your brain and your nervous system during deep sleep. Getting good sleep is one of the best and most natural ways to assure yourself a good even performance in your sport and other areas of life.

To assure a good night's sleep you shouldn't eat heavily before going to sleep. Also, before going to sleep, think positive thoughts about yourself, about your day, and about the activities you'll be performing the next day. In this way, you will wake up with a positive attitude toward your day.

Although you may think that watching TV or a video is a relaxing pastime that will prepare you for a good night's sleep, be careful of the type of movies you watch. A late night suspense, action or horror movie can do more to prevent a good night's sleep than to provide one. Keeping your mood positive with your family will also help you to rest more easily. What you put into your mind as well as what you put into your body has a great effect on the quality of your sleep. *Imagine a future in which you feel mentally, physically and emotionally strong because you can count on your excellent sleep habits to provide you with the energy that you need.*

Remember how valuable a good peaceful night's sleep is to keep your energy consistent in your sport and in your life.

~ Garo's Guidelines ~

*One likes to 'hang out',
drink, smoke,
and use drugs to make him feel good.*

*The other likes to feel good naturally,
work hard and play hard,
and go for the best possible result.*

*If you had to put your life
in the hands of one of these two people,
which one would it be?*

*As you are growing
and taking charge of your own life,
what do <u>you</u> want to be?*

*Stay away from bad habits and
be happy and successful . . .*

. . . naturally.

WHEN YOU FEEL GOOD 'NATURALLY' . . .

When you feel good naturally, without the need for alcohol, drugs, tobacco, etc . . . you'll enjoy your sport more and feel better about life in general. Here's why:

If you use alcohol, it 'appears' to relax you and lower your stress. But when the effects wear off, you have less ability to handle stress and you become more tense and nervous. So using alcohol to have a good time doesn't work. It can start a downward trend in your life. To have a good time, you can just laugh more, be with people who make your laugh, and enjoy your own sense of humor. Laughter provides a much better stress release than alcohol and it actually strengthens your body rather than weakening it. Drugs that make you appear to feel stronger, more confident or more focused will have the same consequence as alcohol. After the effects wear off they will make it more difficult to concentrate, and they will reduce your confidence because you'll need something to make you feel strong and confident.

Stimulants, alcohol, drugs, tobacco, even too much caffeine can be a real trap for the young athlete. If you use it to feel 'up', then after (when you 'come down') you'll need more to feel good again. Because you want to continue with good performance, you'll keep taking it until your body eventually shuts down and you lose everything. The answer is simply not to start. If you've started, ask advice from someone you trust on how to begin reducing or stop. A good thing to remember is that our bodies produce natural chemicals that make us feel good when we exercise, laugh, eat good foods and get good rest and sleep. *Imagine a future in which you feel naturally strong because you can count on your nutrition, exercise and sleep habits to provide you with the energy that you need.*

Remember that your body can produce all it needs to keep you feeling your best.

- Garo's Guidelines -

*The best athletes are tough and strong
on the outside,
and relaxed on the inside.*

*The 'coolest' people
are effective on the outside
and relaxed on the inside.*

*Making time for relaxation
(like anything else)
is a habit.*

*Everyday get into the habit
of taking just a few moments
to do something
that relaxes you naturally.*

*Do this day-by-day,
week-by-week,
and life will just get easier and easier*

WHEN YOU MAKE TIME FOR RELAXATION . . .

When you make time for relaxation . . . you are learning a habit that will make your athletic performance and your life stronger and more enjoyable. Here's how this valuable habit works to improve your life:

Your very best performance starts with a feeling of being loose, relaxed and alert. This feeling lets you arouse your body to its best performance when you need it. If you are stressed, it means that you are already aroused and you might easily become over-aroused or too aroused in your playing. If you are over-aroused, you find it hard to focus and to control your performance. That's why learning how to relax can work wonders for your athletic performance.

Let's start with the basic question: What is stress? Well, in normal everyday activities, you exert your muscles, and they tense and relax naturally. When your muscles feel tense even when you are not intentionally exerting yourself, it means that you are 'stressed'. There are different ways that you can relieve stress and let your muscles relax. These include sleep and naps, pleasant daydreaming, listening to music, taking a walk, or a pastime that gives you good feelings. You may have your own stress relieving activities that you're naturally using in your own life.

Learning to relax has many benefits. When you are relaxed, your outlook is calmer, you are more effective, you enjoy what you are doing and you tend to look for the fun in life. Relaxing will also improve your nutrition because you won't be eating out of a stress habit. *Imagine a future in which you feel mentally, physically and emotionally strong because you can count on your relaxation habits to provide you with the energy that you need.*

Strive to stay in that natural relaxed and alert feeling in your sport and your everyday activities.

~ Garo's Guidelines ~

*Here's a great habit to form
in your life:*

*Every day look for
at least one good thing about someone
you see or meet.*

*One a day,
seven days a week
is 365 things a year.*

*How do you think this will make you feel
about people,
about life,
about yourself?*

*Start right now.
Think of someone you met today
and name a good thing about them.
Then make it a habit!*

WHEN YOU LOOK FOR
THE GOOD IN PEOPLE . . .

When you look for the good in people . . . you are developing an outlook that will bring you happiness in your relationships and your life. Here's how it works:

Your sport is a great place to look for the good in people because it's easy to know what it means to be good in a sport- a good arm - being quick on your feet, etc. Get in the habit of spotting skill and talent and feeling genuinely good for the person who has it. This outlook will allow you to more easily talk about your own skills and talent in a positive way, which will help you to present yourself well throughout your life.

Your sport is also a place where good and bad *traits* come out in people. The good includes things like sportsmanship, humility, enthusiasm, toughness and courage. The bad might include things like anger, jealousy, cheating or fighting. Because of this, your sport is a great place to develop the ability to focus on the positive in people. Since there will always be good and bad in the world, it is your choice where you want to focus. Usually what you look for is what you'll find. When you focus on the good, you'll find good. When you focus on the bad, you'll find bad. If you focus on the bad, you'll come to believe that people in general are bad, and treat them as though they're not to be trusted. Then they will feel this, and your negative attitude <u>will</u> bring out the bad in them - all because you chose to see the bad in them instead of the good. When you see people as good, you trust people. They sense this, and your positive attitude will bring out the good in them. *Imagine a future in which you bring out the best in people because of your positive outlook.*

Remember if you want good things to happen in your life, begin to focus on the good you see around you. A great place to start is in your sport and with the important people in all areas of your life. You can start by thinking of all the people you know only in terms of their positive qualities.

~ Garo's Guidelines ~

Whether it's when you
first open your eyes in the morning,
when your feet first hit the floor,
when you brush your teeth,
or when you're having breakfast,

get into the habit every morning
to take a moment to tell yourself

that you're claiming the day ahead of you
as your own,

that you will make the very most of it,

and you will expect the best
from everyone
who is part of your day.

WHEN YOU EXPECT THE BEST FROM OTHERS . . .

When you expect the best from others . . . you are developing an essential leadership skill that you can use to help others in your sport and all the people in your life. Let's take a closer look:

When someone knows that you are expecting them to be their best, it adds to their motivation because you are adding more 'want' to something that *they already want.* One way of developing this trait is to give the best of yourself. The more you give your best, the more you'll expect the best from others. With this positive attitude, you will want to play with people who are at your own level of skill to improve both yourself and the others involved. Realize that if the other person doesn't have the knowledge, skills or traits to play at your level, your positive expectancy will not work. In this case you would be helping them by expecting them to practice harder and prepare to play at your level.

What's in it for you when you expect others to be their best? When you expect the best from others you are saying that you first expect the best from yourself. By doing this, you will strive to be your best.

Your friendships, school life and family life will also benefit from this positive trait. One of the genuine signs of friendship is expecting your friend to be their best. In family life, there is no greater motivation for a boy or girl than the positive expectation from their big brother or sister. In work or career leadership, positive expectancy is an essential trait.. Once a manager assigns a task to someone, expecting them to follow through plays a big part in making it happen. *Imagine a future in which you can draw on the power of positive expectancy whenever you are called to leadership.*

Learn to expect the best from others and you will find it easier to bring out the best in yourself.

~ Garo's Guidelines ~

We're all students of life.

When you learn something well enough,
you might want to find people
who also want to learn it,
and help them.

Even though you will be acting
as a teacher,
see yourself as a student
who has learned something
and is sharing your knowledge.

The person with the true
champion spirit
looks for opportunities
to help others
with the gifts they have been given.

WHEN YOU HELP SOMEONE . . .

When you help someone . . . you are getting 'out of yourself' and into the needs of another person. Here's why helping others is such a great quality.

When you give yourself totally in your athletic performance, something magical happens. Suddenly you get out of your own thoughts - out of your problems - and into the moves and goals of the game. Another good feeling (that gets you out of your own thoughts and problems) happens when you give yourself to help someone. There are many opportunities to have this feeling in your sport and your life. In your sport, you can always help your teammates with encouragement, advice and suggestions. Naturally in your friendships, there are always opportunities to be of help. In your family life, there are opportunities to have this great feeling *everyday*. When you help with household chores, you might want to share your feelings with your parents by saying something like, "I feel good doing this because I know that it's helping you". Volunteering is a great way to *develop new skills* while helping others. Read-a-thons, math-a-thons and other school fundraising programs are other ways to help others.

In the world, when you see such people helping others who are less fortunate, you realize that they see all people as being one big family. As for work life, the true meaning of career and profession is in the purpose of helping others. So by growing in the spirit of helping others, you are preparing for a very personally satisfying work life. *Imagine a future in which people in all areas of your life are benefiting from knowing you.*

The highest awards are given to people because of the good they do in the world - their unselfish service to others. Recognize the ways that you are helping people in your sport and in your life. Remember the good feeling you have when you help others, and keep this feeling alive everyday.

~ Garo's Guidelines ~

*Have a good purpose in your life.
Find something that you feel
you were meant to do.*

*The stronger you feel about it,
the more you'll think about it.*

*The more you think about it,
the more you'll talk about it.*

*The more you talk about it,
the more people will know about it.*

*The more people who know about it,
the more people will offer to help.*

*In this way, your purpose will grow
and you will enjoy success,
especially if your purpose itself
involves helping others.*

WHEN YOU ARE BEING HELPED BY SOMEONE...

When you are being helped by someone . . . you are learning a lesson that will give you a great advantage in your life. Let's take a closer look:

When you play a sport, you are in a situation where people are continually offering to help you in one way or another. Coaches, assistant coaches, your parents, older and more experienced athletes will come to your assistance to help you in your sport. Some athletes *won't accept* help because they have a negative type of pride. They think they have to prove that they can do it on their own. Other athletes have personal problems and feel that they *can't be* helped. The answer in this case is for them to get in touch with their true feelings and share them with someone they trust. Some people feel they don't *deserve* help. This could be because they don't have the natural feeling themselves to help others. This may come from having been hurt in their life, and now they just don't feel like helping someone else. If you feel this way, realize that the people who hurt you were just a few people. There are many other people out there who want to help. When you get into the habit of helping people, you'll become more aware that there are good people in the world and that you're becoming one of them. You'll feel like you are part of a club - part of the good 'force' in the world, and you'll accept help more easily.

In other areas of life, help is available. In school, your teacher, school counselor, older students, are there to help. Your parents are there for you. Relatives, friends and neighbors will help when they know what you need. *Imagine a future in which people are continually coming to your assistance to help you reach your goals.*

Be tough with yourself when you develop your skills and reach your goals. Be easy on yourself by accepting the help that people are offering.

~ Garo's Guidelines ~

*Think of something in your life
that you want to achieve.*

*Now think of someone
who also wants to achieve the same goal.*

Suggest to work on it together.

Ask yourself,

*"Do I want this
as much as my friend wants it?"*

*The answer to this question will
help you to either*

*strengthen your own performance
or
inspire your friend to strengthen theirs.*

WHEN YOU 'BUDDY' WITH SOMEONE FOR SUCCESS . . .

When you buddy with someone for success . . . you are learning the true meaning of partnership. Here's how partnering will help you in your sport and in your life:

In your sport, you might buddy with one or two particular players to develop certain skills. There also might be players who are similar to you in other ways, so you feel comfortable sharing your thoughts and feelings and other parts of your life. When you buddy with someone in this way you are adding something valuable to your sport. Besides feeling like a friendship is coming out of your sport, you also begin to feel like your sport is part of your friendship. In other words, as a friend you want the player or teammate to get better in their sport. Hoping for the best for someone is a true mark of friendship. In this way, your sport is a great place to build true friendships based on helping each other.

When you bring this feeling into your school life, you start to buddy with classmates to succeed in your education. Doing homework together or sharing in a school project can be ways to partner for success in your school life. When you share chores at home, you are buddying in your family. Your family life, just like your sport and your education, has very clear goals - meals, laundry, cleaning up, etc. In your friendships, you are buddying in other ways that include learning together and just having fun together. As you begin to form lasting relationships in your life, this partnership quality will help you greatly. In your career or professional life, you will naturally learn how to choose the right people to assure success for all involved. *Imagine a future in which you have partners in all areas of life with whom you share success and happiness.*

Realize that most of your goals in life will be reached with the help of others. Learn the value of partnership now and your life will be more fun and so much easier.

~ Garo's Guidelines ~

*If today,
anyone did something
that bothered you,
or hurt you,
or made you feel bad,*

*tonight,
before you go to sleep
think back on your day
and say something like the following:*

*"Before I go to sleep
I am letting go of any bad feelings
people may have caused me today.
I am a forgiving person."*

*When you empty yourself of bad feelings,
you will start filling yourself
with good feelings.*

WHEN YOU FORGIVE SOMEONE . . .

When you forgive someone . . . you are doing something very special *for yourself* as well as for the other person. Here's why:

Sometime in your sport, someone might do something that makes you feel upset or angry with them. You might feel like they've done something wrong *to you personally*. This is the time to realize that errors don't only occur in your sport, but also in the way that people treat others. Think about it, when someone makes an error in a game, how do you feel? Does their error make you feel bad about yourself as a person? Probably not. Treat people who make errors in their behavior the same way. Hopefully the person who makes the 'social' error will learn by their mistake and grow personally just as they are growing in their athletic skills.

If someone does something wrong to you, you might think that forgiving them means 'letting them off the hook'. A better way to think about forgiveness is that you are letting go of a bad feeling that you are having. If the feeling isn't useful to you, just let it go.

Since these kinds of 'errors' or misunderstandings occur in all areas of life, forgiveness is a very valuable personal quality to develop. In school, family, and especially friendships, you can benefit by practicing forgiveness to let go of negative feelings. In your future career or profession it will be important to let go of negative feelings so they don't interfere with your performance. By developing this very important quality of forgiveness now, it will feel easier and more natural as you grow into adulthood. *Imagine a future in which negative feelings have no power over you, and you are free to create and maintain positive feelings.*

Remember, forgiveness is the first step in learning to be emotionally strong in all areas of life.

~ Garo's Guidelines ~

*If you choose to go along with the crowd,
when you know it's wrong,
you may not lose their friendship
but you'll never win self-respect either.*

*You'll just always be watching others,
thinking about others,
talking about others,
following others.*

*When you decide to start playing
your own winning game,
you'll either help
to turn your friends into winners,
or you'll leave the group of losers
and be glad that you're no longer one of them.*

*Play to win in the game of life.
Don't let any group make you lose
by doing what you <u>know</u> is not right <u>for you</u>.*

WHEN YOU HANDLE PEER PRESSURE . . .

When you handle peer pressure and do what you know is right . . . you are preparing for personal leadership in your life. Here's more about it:

When friends get together, it's like being in a team. All of your friends have a true sense of what is good performance. For example, everyone knows that smoking cigarettes does serious damage to your body. It's a proven fact. If one of your friends smokes, they are making an 'error' in the game of life. If that person influences other kids, it's like an athlete (who makes errors) telling the rest of the team that it's 'cool' to make errors. To handle peer pressure, know why the weak behavior is not really fun and what kind of behavior is fun. For example, if someone is trying to persuade you to smoke, know the facts about smoking. If you know someone who died a painful death from lung cancer or a cigarette-related disease, tell your story (or your reason for not smoking). Another harmful type of peer pressure is when you feel forced to do something that hurts other people (or to think badly of other people). Whatever the weak behavior is, have your own personal reason for not doing it, and stick to it. Also, plan things that are fun and that will be good for you and your friends. Stay true to yourself and maybe your example will help your friends to get out of their weak behavior.

In career or professional life, people sometimes allow themselves to be influenced by people who don't like their work. They then wind up being unhappy themselves in their work. Begin to strengthen yourself now. *Imagine a future in which you won't be influenced to think or behave in ways that will weaken you.*

Realize that peer pressure is probably the most challenging social situation in a person's life. When you handle it and you still feel good about life and about yourself, you deserve the biggest trophy in the game of life.

– Garo's Guidelines –

*When there's a problem,
sometimes you just have to listen to*

*what the other person wants,
why they want it,
why they think they deserve it,
what they are feeling,
what they are <u>really</u> saying.*

*When you do this as a true friend,
in an honest way,
there is a very good chance
that they will listen to*

*what you want,
why you want it,
why you think you deserve it,
what you are feeling,
what you are <u>really</u> saying.*

Problem solved!

WHEN YOU HAVE A PROBLEM WITH SOMEONE...

When you have a problem with someone . . . you can learn a valuable lesson about people. Here's more about turning a problem into an advantage:

In your sport, you meet all kinds of people and they're all there for the same purpose. In this way, they're all the same. In another way, all the people are different, and that's in their personalities and points-of-view. When people with different points-of-view play or work together, disagreements happen and problems can occur. Whenever you have a problem with someone, first realize that it is because you have different points-of-view about something. The very first thing is to understand 'where they're coming from'. Once you try to understand them, you might even find that you agree with them. If you don't agree with their point-of-view, respect that they have the right to their own opinion.

Your sport is a good place to start working on these important skills (understanding others and having others understand you). Your school is another place where there are a lot of people with different points-of-view. In your friendships, you'll see that friendship is really all about sharing interests, activities, goals, attitudes and feelings

One of the worst problems between people is *prejudice* - where one kind of people resist another. Bring your skills into your future and use understanding to reduce prejudice between people whenever you have the opportunity. In your future career or profession, you'll find that the ability to resolve problems between people is regarded as a very valuable skill. *Imagine a future in which your understanding leads to great friendships, relationships and success.*

Remember that people are the cause of 'people problems'. Understand yourself and then strive to understand others and you'll have rewarding relationships.

~ Garo's Guidelines ~

A Parent Problem List

You feel they are unfair.
You don't feel like you can confide in them.
Your parents get in the middle of trouble with a brother or sister.
They're watching you so closely.
They're pressuring or expecting you to do too much.
They're not giving you privacy or independence.
You want to feel closer with your parent(s).
You want to have more time with them.
They don't understand you.
You want to be more understanding of them.

Suggestion

Ask them
how they handled the problem
when <u>they</u> were young.

WHEN YOU HAVE A PROBLEM WITH YOUR PARENTS . . .

When you have a problem with your parent(s) . . . you have a chance to learn one of the most important lessons of your life. Let's take a closer look at this unique learning experience:

In many way, parents are the most important people in a young person's life. Because of this, when we begin to have problems with our parents, it can be very challenging. There are different kinds of problems that young people can have with their parents. In sports, a young person can feel like their parents: aren't interested enough, are too hard on them or are too concerned about them getting hurt. Each of these things affect how we see ourselves. If we think they're not interested, we might begin to feel unimportant. If we think they are too hard on us, we might feel like we're not good enough. If we think they're too concerned, we might begin to feel afraid of confronting challenges. Realize that parents are only doing what they think is best for you.

The best way to resolve a problem with your parents is to talk with them. Be sure to talk with them respectfully, but be sure to *make your point*. Don't forget that your parents have made so many decisions for you that it might be hard for them to accept your way of thinking. Because of this, you might have to repeat your message a number of times. By learning to resolve problems with your parents, you are learning to communicate effectively with people in challenging situations. *Imagine a future in which you can resolve 'people problems' and genuinely enjoy being with people.*

Remember, parents are people just like you. They had the same problems as you when they were growing up. With this in mind, see them as friends with similar problems . . . and talk with them as you would talk with a trusted friend about problems. This outlook should make it a lot easier.

~ Garo's Guidelines ~

*Feel that enthusiasm,
that forward-moving energy,
that confidence,
that sureness,*

*and let this feeling come through
in your sports performance.*

*Don't let anyone
stop,
block
or bring down
this powerful feeling
with petty words, looks or gestures.*

*Realize that they are
revealing their own weakness,
and use this to focus <u>even more</u>
on your strengths.*

WHEN YOU ARE BEING 'PSYCHED OUT' . . .

When someone is trying to psyche you out . . . you have a great opportunity to build your strength, determination and concentration. Let's look at this a little closer:

When someone's trying to psyche you out, it simply means that they don't feel they have enough athletic skill to compete with you and they need to use other tactics. A person may try to make you feel: *fear* with unnecessary roughness or the threat of it, *worried* about some advantage they have over you, *inferior* to them by pointing out the ways they are superior to you, *unworthy* as an athlete by joking about your performance, *unimportant* by totally ignoring you, *distracted* by pointing out difficulties in the game, *inferior* by continually talking about themselves, about their game, about how good they are, *self-conscious* by flattering you, or some other way of 'putting the spotlight on you'. The self-conscious psyche-out is the worst because it makes you consciously focus on all your skills and moves that should be instinctive. This puts you into the feeling that you are back in a beginning stage of your learning (where mistakes are often made). Others may even find ways of making you feel sorry for them, or guilty, or laxed in your performance. Be aware that if a person's words or manner are affecting your performance, it could be a psyche-out.

The solution is to become aware of these tactics and use them as challenges to developing mental and emotional toughness. Handling psyche-outs in your sport is an excellent way to prepare for psyche-out artists in life (when they can do a good deal of damage if you let them). *Imagine a future in which you can respond effectively to <u>all</u> kinds of people.*

Remember, when you effectively handle psyche-outs and remain strong and focused, you go beyond your athletic skill development to a higher level of mental and emotional toughness.

~ Garo's Guidelines ~

*Seeing other people behave badly
(especially if they're adults)
can give us mixed feelings,
and make us unsure of exactly <u>what</u> to feel.*

*The most important thing to remember
if you see people behaving badly
is to never let their behavior
make you,
in any way,
feel bad about yourself.*

*Just be <u>you</u>,
behave in a way
that makes you feel strong within yourself,
and avoid behavior
that can make you feel weak.*

WHEN YOU SEE PEOPLE BEHAVING BADLY . . .

When you see people behaving badly . . . you have a valuable opportunity to learn something about human nature. Let's take a look:

When athletes have a challenge in their sport, either they can look at it clearly and work through it calmly, or they can become doubtful or afraid and handle it with frustration (or even anger). When people have challenges in life, they react the same way. Some people handle their problems calmly and some get upset. If a person grew up seeing their relatives and friends often getting upset, they might learn to handle their problems in the same way. So when you see people behaving badly, realize that it is often some way of handling <u>their own</u> problems in life. It's not about you personally, unless you did something wrong to them. If you did something wrong, you should apologize. If not, realize that the bad behavior is a part of <u>their</u> personality or temperament.

In family, friendships and school, we sometimes see people behaving badly because they don't know how to handle situations. In the world, we see it in things like prejudice against someone's race or religion. If you watch or read the news, you'll see examples every day of people behaving <u>very</u> badly, committing crimes against others. Unfortunately, the news often stresses the bad. So it can be very challenging to watch the news and stay in an optimistic mood. The solution is to treat these bad 'feelings' as a distraction (similar to a distraction in your game). In other words, win the inner game of life by always returning your focus to the good in life. *Imagine a future in which you can effectively handle the bad you see in the world, and help to create more good.*

Remember when you see people behaving badly, use it to strengthen your determination to stay focused on the good. Bring this focus into your friendships and family, and use it contribute to making things better in your world.

- Garo's Guidelines -

*Successful people always
have stories, ideas, beliefs,
and principles
that they have lived by
to reach their success*

*One belief
shared by all successful people
is that to be successful,
you must learn
to work well with people.*

*Make this idea your own,
live by it,
and you will be one of those successful people
sharing the secrets of <u>your</u> success
with others.*

WHEN YOU WORK WELL WITH OTHERS . . .

When you work well with others . . . you are preparing for a life of success and happiness because both success and happiness are the result of things like cooperation and partnership. Here's more:

One of the most enjoyable things about team sports is the very fact that you are playing with a team. With this in mind, you can see that there are *two* reasons for developing your athletic skills - to express your own ability, and to have the opportunity to perform your skills with others. In your future you'll find that many, (if not most) of your activities are things that you will be doing with other people. Ask your parents or another adult how they spend most of their day and you'll find that their activities are in some way performed with other people. Your sport is a great place to prepare for working with others on common goals because: 1) it has a purpose (the sport itself), 2) it has goals (score and specific improvement goals), 3) it has a structure (the practice and the game), and 4) it has roles (players, positions, coaches, officials, etc.).

By working well on common goals, we naturally focus more on our similarities than on our differences. This helps us to accept and appreciate our differences more - differences such as: race (where people look different and may have different ways of thinking, speaking and behaving) and religion (where people have different beliefs). Naturally your ability to work well with others will be very valuable in your future career or profession, since so much of your work life will involve the people you work with, the people you work for, and the people you serve. *Imagine a future in which all the work you do with others is effective and personally rewarding.*

Remember that the better you work with people, the higher will be your success in life. Begin now by genuinely enjoying the people involved in your sport.

~ Garo's Guidelines ~

Here's an interesting fact of life:
Your performance will always reflect your thoughts, feelings and attitude.

With this knowledge,
you can be a mind reader!

Watch a person's performance and you'll know how they're thinking, feeling and what kind of attitude they have!

And you'll soon realize that having an 'up' attitude gets better results than a 'down' attitude.

To have your best performance, go in with an optimistic attitude.

WHEN YOU ARE OPTIMISTIC . . .

When you are optimistic . . . you will find success and happiness wherever you look. Here's how and why optimism works:

When you watch the greatest athletes play, you can see a look of readiness and optimism in their eyes. Optimism is a magic quality. It comes from having faith: 1) faith that what you are doing is a good thing, 2) faith that you are able to do it, and 3) faith that good things will naturally happen for a good person. One of the reasons that optimism works so well is that it makes you feel ready to <u>accept</u> the best things in life. Success opens you to new experiences in life. Some people have a fear of the new and unknown things that success can bring, and therefore, they hold themselves back. When you are optimistic, you naturally can handle success, because you will continue to expect good things to happen after you succeed.

Optimism is a valuable quality in all areas of life because all areas have goals. When you bring a sense of optimism into your family, friendships and school life, your world seems much brighter. More becomes possible. The optimism you develop now will also help you to make positive changes in the world as you grow, because you will want the best for your community, your state, your country and your world. In career and professional life, there is always a focus on achieving the best possible results. Developing the quality of optimism now will prepare you for this area of life. *Imagine a future in which all the good things of life come to you naturally because you expect them and are willing to accept them into your life.*

Keep in mind the *good* reason behind what you're doing. Strive to be *good* at what you're doing. Expect *good* things to happen and look for ways to <u>make them happen</u>. There is *goodness* in our world and you are part of it.

- Garo's Guidelines -

If I could either have more talent or more toughness, I'd choose more toughness.

It is a known fact that athletes with a little talent and a lot of toughness

will always do better than

athletes with a lot of talent and little toughness.

Get tough . . .
. . . and stay tough!

WHEN YOU ARE TOUGH...

When you are tough in your sport . . . you are preparing to handle the challenges of life and be a true 'winner'. Here's more about developing toughness:

Toughness is such a powerful quality that with it, you can even accomplish more than people who have greater talent and skill than you have. We've all been born with a certain amount of *talent*. Talent is a natural gift each of us has been given. When we develop *skills*, we are using our talent and improving it. When we become *tough*, it means we have found a way to perform at our best or very near our best, no matter how the competition is playing or how the game is going. What does it feel like when you're performing at your best? You feel <u>ready</u> - ready for the challenge, ready for the competition. So the key to getting tough is to put yourself in this great feeling of being ready to compete and to enjoy the competition. The best way to develop toughness is simply to practice *being tough*. Begin by thinking tough, acting tough and feeling tough. To think tough, think 'I can do it' thoughts. To act tough, carry yourself in a way that shows you're confident, relaxed, energized and ready for the competition. To feel tough, get to that feeling that you are undefeatable, that no matter what happens, you'll remain strong and keep giving your best. Then put yourself into the action and see if you really are tough.

Your home life, with its chores and responsibilities is a great place to build toughness. Do a hard chore just to <u>*prove*</u> your toughness and see what it feels like. *Imagine a future in which you actually enjoy the challenges of life because you are tough and ready for them.*

Challenge yourself mentally, emotionally and physically in all areas of your life and build your toughness to handle challenges   The tougher *you* get, the more fun *it* gets.

~ Garo's Guidelines ~

*The athlete
who needs to be the star of the game
is just interested in his own glory.*

*The true star
is the athlete who knows
that most of the work
is done behind the scenes,*

*doing those little things
day-by-day
that build and strengthen
character.*

*Be a true star
of your own life,
and the recognition you receive
in your sport
will take care of itself.*

WHEN YOU ARE HUMBLE IN YOUR ACCOMPLISHMENTS...

74

When you are humble in your accomplishments . . . you find yourself accomplishing more. Here's why being humble is such a strong success trait:

To be humble is to realize that you have been given certain talents and to be deeply grateful for them. Being humble is *a strength* since it shows that you feel so good about yourself that you don't have to try to prove it to others by bragging about yourself. If someone is good (or even very good) at their sport and they need to brag about it, it means that they are not yet 'great'. Greatness comes when the athlete shows more focus on the larger purpose of the sport than on the individual concerns of his or her own recognition. The humble athlete is truly playing the 'inner game' because they are more focused on their development in their sport and the kind of personal growth that will contribute to improved performance.

Having a sense of humility also will improve your social life. If you are ego-centered, people will realize that you're more concerned with yourself, which doesn't make for good relationships. If you're humble, people realize that you can get out of yourself and into the lives of other people. You can be genuinely happy for them. In career and professional life, it is generally known that the humble person who 'gets the job done' is the most successful) or on their way to being the most successful). *Imagine a future in which you are so accomplished that people recognize it naturally.*

Keep up the good work, my friend. Remember to just keep giving your best effort and focus on steady improvement. In this way, you won't feel the need to brag . . . you'll just feel naturally good about yourself.

- Garo's Guidelines -

Bring your feeling
of doubt
to
0%

by
bringing your feeling
of confidence
to
100%

There are three ways to do this:

1. Practice
2. Practice
3. Practice

WHEN YOU ARE CONFIDENT IN THE FACE OF DOUBT . . .

When you remain confident in the face of doubt . . . you are at the very top of your game. Here's how overcoming doubt works in your sport and in life:

When a game begins, whether it's a little league game or a professional championship game, nobody knows for sure who is going to win. If an athlete knew for sure that he or she was going to win, it would no longer be 'a game'. Although an athlete can't know in their mind that they're going to win, they can *know in their heart* that they're going to win. This feeling develops when you learn to build your confidence in the face of doubt. When you begin your sport, you don't have many skills, so you use your desire to play and your faith in your ability to make you feel confident. As you learn what is expected of you, you use this desire to reach your goals and to overcome doubts. As you develop your skills and you begin achieving more, you add more confidence to your playing. When people recognize your talents, this recognition builds even more confidence. With each of these stages, your doubt decreases until you feel no doubt - no fear - and you play with total confidence.

We have doubts in all areas of life, so this positive quality will naturally overlap into your school life, social life and family life. Learning to build and maintain your confidence now will greatly help you in your future career or professional life. *Imagine a future in which self-doubt cannot weaken you because you know how to remain confident in the face of doubt.*

If you're just beginning in your sport, draw confidence from your desire to play. If you're further along in your sport, also draw confidence from your skills and your accomplishments. Whenever any kind of doubt appears in your life, look for the confidence that will reduce or remove it.

- Garo's Guidelines -

Outer Competition

*Competing
against
the opposing team.*

Inner Competition

*"The athlete
you are today"
competing with
"the athlete
you were yesterday".*

*Inner competition
is the best way to win the
outer competition.*

WHEN YOU ARE COURAGEOUS IN COMPETITION . . .

When you are courageous in competition . . . you are preparing to actually enjoy the challenges of life. Let's see how:

When you go into an unknown situation, such as doing something you've never done, reaching for a new level of playing skill or approaching a very challenging task, it is courage that you rely on to handle the situation. When you show courage it means that you feel sure of yourself, you expect the best from yourself and you 'go for it' in the face of great challenge. When you and your team are courageous it means that you are aggressively setting the pace for the game and that the other team has to play up to you. You move ahead strongly and confidently without a thought of defeat. You enjoy the competition and you look forward to situations and plays that test your courage. Developing courage is one of the greatest benefits of being in a sport. Since courage is a test of how you handle challenges, the greater the challenge the better the opportunity to develop and strengthen your courage. So instead of looking for the easy way out, look for the greater challenges and enjoy greater satisfaction when you reach your goals.

With the courage you develop in your sport, you will look forward to the challenges in other areas of your life. With courage, you will 'go for it' and 'make it happen' in your school life, your family life and later on within your career or profession. *Imagine a future in which you have the courage to go for the higher challenges and make great things happen.*

Remember that courage will open doors for you in all areas of your life . . . and then with even more courage, you will confidently walk through those doors.

= Garo's Guidelines =

*There is something
within each one of us
that knows the exact right answer
to the 'important' questions in life*

It's called our 'conscience'.

*Once we're in touch with it
and are guided by it,
all of our decisions
are the right decisions.*

*Once we accept it,
we understand that having rules
is what keeps
the fairness in games,
as well as in groups of people.*

WHEN YOU PLAY BY THE RULES . . .

When you play by the rules . . . you are developing a trait that will assure success in your life. Here's why following rules is a 'guaranteed' success trait:

Do you know how your sport began? It began with people enjoying the activities such as throwing, catching, running, passing, hitting or whatever activities make up your sport. Then someone thought is would be a good idea to turn it into 'a game' so people could have more fun by competing. With competition, players got better, and today there are great athletes in your sport. This all became possible because people agreed on certain things that could and couldn't be done while playing - these agreements are called *the rules*.

The first thing you look for when you play a game is the fun you'll have. Next you look for the object (the goal) of the game. Then you learn the rules of the game. For people who are happy and successful, life itself is like a game. There are opportunities to have fun and to learn in all areas of life, and there are goals . . . and rules. In school there are rules that allow entire classrooms of students to work together to learn and have fun. Family life is a great experience when you live by certain rules. There are also rules that friends follow with each other in order to be true friends. Learning to play by rules now will make it easier in your future work life, where accepting and following rules bring success. Society has rules called *laws*. By agreeing to live by laws, we can have very large groups of people living and working together in a positive way. We call these groups our neighborhoods, towns, cities and states. *Imagine a future in which the rules make it easier for you to win, because you genuinely like playing by rules.*

Remember that you have to follow rules to play . . . and you have to play to win. Play by the rules and win 'the inner game' in all areas of your life.

~ Garo's Guidelines ~

*One friend
tells you how great he is,
trying to prove something about himself
and doing very little to actually prove it.*

*Another
goes about his business,
applying himself,
just being himself and acting naturally,*

*getting the job done,
without saying much about it,
and letting his results do the talking.*

Which one is 'cool'?

Which would you rather be?

WHEN YOU ARE 'COOL'...

When you are cool . . . you feel natural, loose, relaxed, and effective. What more can you say about being 'cool'? Let's take a look:

In some ways, being cool means the same thing for everybody. In some ways it means something totally different. All cool people feel okay with themselves, accept themselves for who they are and seem happy with themselves. But all cool people don't have the same personality. In other words, coolness has nothing to do with your personality. It's about *how you feel* about your personality. When you're loose, relaxed and positive in your sport, you'll play well. When you feel this way in your life, you're cool.

Another way of saying you're cool is to say that you have a personal *style*. When you feel okay with yourself, you let your natural style or manner express itself. You don't try to be like other people who are 'thought to be' cool. Trying to be like someone else is 'uncool' because you're saying that it's not enough just to be you. Naturally, having a positive personal style or manner will benefit you in other areas of your life. When you accept yourself within your friendships, your family and your school life, you enjoy life more. People will be more comfortable in your company because you feel comfortable in your own company. Take a look at your personality - your interests, activities, your feelings, your goals, what you like to talk about, how you are with people. Be okay with all these positive things about yourself. You don't need approval to like yourself,. you can give yourself approval. *Imagine a future in which you wake up every morning feeling good about yourself . . . and feeling great about life.*

Take that loose, relaxed, good feeling that you have when you're playing well and make it a part of your everyday life.

- Garo's Guidelines -

*Whatever you do in your life,
claim it to be you own.
Make it personal.*

*Whether or not you win the exact result
that you want,
at the very least,
win the moment <u>for yourself</u>.*

*One way you can lose the moment
is by letting anger take over.*

Make it personal but don't overheat.

*Anger just costs too much energy -
energy that you can be focusing
on your performance instead.*

WHEN YOU FEEL THE URGE TO GET ANGRY . . .

When you feel the urge to get angry . . . you have the opportunity to take control of the most powerful force of human nature - your emotions. Let's take a closer look:

When you can't handle a challenge with your skills, you might choose to handle it with your emotions. If you are willing to 'go for it', the emotion that you use might be anger because anger can stir up an aggression toward your goal that will keep you moving toward it. Although anger can be useful in this way, it should always be the last resort and should be avoided if at all possible. It is an 'expensive' emotion because it uses a great deal of energy that would be better used for productive concentrated effort. It is usually undependable and often uncontrollable. If you feel the urge to get angry, see if it's because you can't handle the challenge with your skills. If you still feel anger coming on and you can't figure it out, channel the energy of your anger into a positive use. Your sport is a great place to learn to deal with anger because you can channel its energy into directed physical activities.

When you are angry *with someone*, you are usually unhappy with something about yourself and you are directing your feeling toward someone else. It could be that someone did something to you that you don't know how to handle or that doesn't make sense to you. Realize that becoming angry is something you are *choosing to do* and that you can choose to remain calm and learn from the experience instead. Bring this realization into other areas of your life and create a more peaceful feeling in your family life, school life and friendships. *Imagine a future in which you are using all of your energy toward reaching your goals because you have learned not to waste energy with anger.*

Keep in mind how much energy it takes to become angry and choose to use your energy for a more constructive use whenever possible.

~ Garo's Guidelines ~

*If you ask people
what they want out of life,
they might tell you what they want to <u>have</u>.*

*If you then ask them
what they <u>really</u> want out of life
they may tell you what they want to <u>do</u>.*

*If you ask people
what they <u>really personally</u> want out of life
they might tell you what they want to <u>feel</u>.*

*Most people
want to feel good about themselves.*

*When you've made a mistake
that is making you feel bad about yourself,
allow yourself to be forgiven.*

*After all, you're human
just like the rest of us.*

WHEN YOU ALLOW
YOURSELF TO BE FORGIVEN . . .

When you allow yourself to be forgiven . . . you are admitting a mistake, which is a first step in correcting it (and learning from it). This is an essential trait to reach success and happiness in life. Here's more about it:

We usually think of mistakes as something we might make in school or on the playing field, but we can also make mistakes with people and in other personal ways. If we make mistakes that hurt or offend another person, the best thing to do is to ask to be forgiven so you don't carry around bad feelings about yourself. Always remember that allowing yourself to be forgiven (as well as forgiving others) is really about 'letting go' of bad feelings.

What about when we make mistakes that hurt ourselves or damage our own character? For example, when we lie, we are first lying to ourselves. Since this is an action that hurts us personally by damaging our own character, who do we ask to forgive us? If we cheat, we are lying about what we know. Cheating is another way of saying, "I don't feel good enough the way I am, so I have to lie about what I know." When you tell yourself you're not good enough over and over again, you begin to actually believe it. Who do we ask to forgive us for damaging our own character in this way? If you are a religious person or if you attend a regular religious service, you may want to ask God for forgiveness. You might also speak to a counselor about how to 'forgive yourself' for the things you do that may be hurting yourself or damaging your own character. However you do it, it is important to let yourself be forgiven (in any area of your life). *Imagine a future in which you feel <u>truly</u> good about yourself.*

Remember that allowing yourself to be forgiven is necessary if you want to correct certain kinds of mistakes and learn from them.

~ Garo's Guidelines ~

Today you have the opportunity
to 'go for it'
or not to go for it,

to take on a challenge now
or to avoid a challenge,

to put yourself on the line,
or to back away.

At the end of your day,
when you look back,
how will the choice you made
affect your life
and your tomorrow?

Make the right choice!

WHEN YOU 'GO FOR IT', AND HANDLE CHALLENGES NOW . . .

When you 'go for it' and handle your challenges <u>now</u> . . . you are getting a head start in life that will remove or reduce many of the problems that today's adults have. Here's more about it.

When adults have problems, they sometimes think it's because of something that happened to them as a child or teenager. If their parents didn't allow them to do or have something that they really wanted, they think that the experience might have taken away their 'power' to reach goals. If their parents made a decision about them or their family that made them feel unhappy, they think the experience began a pattern of feeling helpless, or even hopeless. Instead of waiting until you're older to look back on your childhood or teenage problems, why not handle them now so they don't grow into bigger challenges. The solution with your parents it to <u>talk with them</u>. If they don't 'get it' or they seem to be blocking your message, put it into other words until they finally understand you. Some adults believe that problems with people come from how they felt about their childhood or teenage friends. Now is the time to develop good relationships in your life. Make sure you have at least one friend with whom you can share your deeper feelings. Adults also believe that a lack of confidence can come from bad feelings they had early in life about mistakes they made. See mistakes in all areas of your life as pointers that show you where you have to improve. This positive way of looking at mistakes will solve this confidence problem. *Imagine a life in which you are free of negativity from your past and can live a totally positive life.*

Realize that your sport is a great place to prepare for a successful and happy future. Share your feelings with your coach and with friends. See mistakes and errors in a positive way. Handle challenges <u>now</u> . . . and enjoy your life!

ABOUT THE "WIN-WIN" BOOK

"WIN-WIN"

A 'Win-Win' happens when two people are playing a 'game' and they <u>both</u> win.

Professional sports trainers say that being an athlete is like being two people who are playing a game with each other. One is the person you are in your sport - your 'role' self. The other is the person you are in your everyday life - your 'real' self. The two are constantly challenging each other, and when one 'wins', the other wins too! In other words, the great thing about being an athlete is that you can use what you learn in your sport to develop good habits and traits, and have success and happiness in your everyday life!

'Winning' in Your Sport

The world's greatest coaches will tell you that they want game victories (and that they plan their entire season to take the championship), but that the *true winner's* day-to-day focus is on things like total personal effort, character, and reaching those small goals toward ongoing improvement.

Winning the Game of Life

The true winner in the game of life has good friends, a happy family life, a sense of purpose in what they do. They stay physically fit. They build their life around positive thoughts, feelings and actions. They know that helping others is the best thing they can do in life.

Use this book regularly and be a 'true winner' in your sport and in your life!

Here's How
The "WIN-WIN" Book Works!

The Right-Side Pages

On each right-side page you'll find a statement at the top that begins with the words, **"When you . . ."**

These statement may concern incidents or events, such as:

"When you win . . .
"When you follow your coach's instructions . . .
"When you make an error . . .

or positive habits, such as:

"When you eat the right foods . . .
"When you play by the rules . . .
"When you look for the good in people . . .

or positive attitudes, such

"When you are tough . . .
"When you are optimistic . . .
"When you are humble in your accomplishments . . .

The topic will be about your development in your sport, your social life or your personal life.

On that page you will discover the benefits of the positive trait or taking positive action in the situation. These benefits include:

- how your performance in your game/sport will improve
- how other areas of your life will *immediately* benefit
- how you are preparing for a successful and enjoyable future

   . . . and other positive benefits

The Left-Side Pages

On the left-side page, you'll find **Garo's Guidelines**. Read this page and be entertained with related insights and suggestions from SuperBowl athlete, Garo Yepremian.

<u>Learning</u> and <u>Fun</u> is what sport (and life) are all about, so we designed this book so that it would give you both!

Garo is totally dedicated to helping young people to develop those positive traits and qualities that will help them succeed in all areas of their lives. Every week he visits schools to share ideas with students of different ages. He teaches with kindness and with humor and always with an eye on practical results . . . and victory. You'll enjoy seeing how Garo turns learning into fun.

(If you look in most library books on football, chances are you'll find Garo's name in them. See our book section titled, 'Garo Yepremian' for more about Garo's sports record and his "Golden Rules in the Sport of Life".)

How to Use The "WIN-WIN" Book

Sometime after your practice or after playing in a game, skim through the book or the chapter index and find a chapter that interests you. By reading just one chapter (5 minutes) after every practice or game, you will begin to see positive changes. The more topics you read, the more positive changes you will see. What's happening is that you are learning from an area of life that you genuinely enjoy - your sport. So it feels good - it feels personal. It builds your dedication to your sport because you realize that your sport is doing so much more for you than you might have ever imagined. While it's helping you to improve your physical skills, it is also bringing certain positive traits and qualities into other areas of your life like your friendships, your education, your family, your self-image (how you feel about yourself), etc.

Another way to use the book is to read about it *before* practice or a game. Pick a topic that is important to you. Then when you find yourself in that situation in your practice or your game, you'll have some insight on a positive way to handle it.

The book has ten parts. Some are directly related to sports, some indirectly related, and some are about social skills, character, self-image and other personal development ideas. Remember that every part of your life affects every other part. When your personal or social life improves, it has an effect on your sport, and when your athletic development improves, it has a positive effect on other areas of your life. You may want to start with topics related to your sport and gradually move into other areas. It's your choice on how you want to use the book. *Just remember that all the ideas in this book will benefit all areas of your life.*

When To Use
The "WIN-WIN" Book

1) As mentioned in the last section, a great time to use the book is after practice or after a game. Just skim through the book or look over the chapter index and find a chapter title that catches your attention. If you won a game that day, you may choose "When You Win . . . ." If you made an error that you feel particularly bad about, you may choose "When You Make An Error . . ."

By reading the "When You" page you'll be using your own experience of that day to teach yourself a valuable lesson - a lesson that will benefit your sport, your life and your future. It works like magic because the idea is directly connected to your own personal experience. After you see this lesson in terms of your own personal experience, wouldn't it be great to see it through the eyes of a professional athlete and learn some guidelines that they discovered in their own experience? On the left-side page, you'll find Garo's Guidelines which will further help you to apply the ideas in the chapter.

2) By reading a chapter before going to sleep, you will go to sleep in a very positive frame of mind. A lot of people believe this is a great way to learn self-improvement ideas because in this very relaxed state you more easily accept positive ideas and make them part of your life.

3) Reading a chapter when you awake in the morning has a very positive effect on your day. By choosing a particular topic, you may actually be preparing to handle something that is happening that day. When you start off in a positive state of mind, you tend to attract positive things into your life.

The main thing to remember is to use the book when *you feel like* using it. This is not homework or an assignment given to you by a teacher or any other authority. It is *your choice* and for your benefit. Treat it that way and you will probably find yourself using it at all different times according to how you feel. Don't make it feel like work. If you make it fun, it will work its magic in your life. You may choose to use it at the same time every day. This has the added benefit that comes from forming a regular positive habit in your life.

Also, instead of just following the advice in this book, once in a while actually take a moment to evaluate the ideas. Judge them for yourself. Read them to personally determine if every idea in the chapter is something that makes sense for you - that you would actually want to make part of your own life. This will make it even more personal for you and it will also make you a stronger and more responsible person.

If you would
like to share
THE "WIN-WIN" BOOK
with your parents,
coaches, teachers,
or other adults
in your life,

ask them to read
the following section!

Dear Parent, Coach or Teacher:

You are reading this section of the "WIN-WIN" Book
because you are personally interested
in the developmental aspect of team sports

and/or

**because a special young athlete
wants to share something important with you -
their interest in achieving
success and happiness in life.**

They also want to feel that they are
helping someone who spends much of their life
helping them.

So on the next page we'll begin with
how this book can help you personally.

If you are an athlete . . .

If you are an athlete, you'll be able to easily translate the principles of the "WIN-WIN" Book into everyday adult situations and see their relevance in your own life, especially in your career or profession. In this way, the book will help you to develop or strengthen the positive traits and qualities in your life - which will benefit your family, your career, and all the areas addressed in the book/program.

If you were a young athlete . . .

If you participated in a team sport as a child or teenager, you can use The "WIN-WIN" Book to recall your early experiences, realize their valuable lessons, and derive the benefits. You will especially enjoy reliving those experiences and discovering new insights about yourself - insights which will help you in all areas of your life.

If you were not involved in a sport . . .

If you were not involved in a team sport as a child or teenager, The "WIN-WIN" book can provide you a with very unique benefit. Many of today's organizations see sports as the basic metaphor for career performance, productivity, and success in general. Those who have not participated in youth sports sometimes feel left out. Since the "WIN-WIN" Book effectively blends sports with success principles, you can begin to understand this sports-success connection and integrate it into your life. One reading will fill in this missing piece of the puzzle in your life.

Dear Parent,

Your son or daughter has shared the "WIN-WIN" Book with you to do you a favor. Thanking your young athlete for the opportunity to read the preceding section will support their own positive self-image. It will also support their ongoing use of the book, which as you can see, will have a long-range positive effect on their life.

Dear Coach or Teacher,

Your young person has shared the 'WIN-WIN" Book with you to do you a favor. Thanking them for the opportunity to read this section will support their own positive self-image. It will also support their ongoing use of the book, which as you can see, will have long range positive effect on their life. As you know, recommending this book to others in the presence of this young athlete or giving this young athlete the opportunity to help others will also strengthen their personal leadership potential.

Now that we've explored
how this book can benefit you personally,
let's take a look at why it is so important
for our young people.

Imagine that every time your young athlete practices or plays their sport, they learn things that we wish we had the opportunity to learn at their age.

Imagine that every time they practice or play in a game, they learn things that so many adults today are paying thousands of dollars to learn, because we never learned them earlier in life.

Today's adults are finding that there are many important things about life that weren't learned in their childhood and teenage years. For this reason, we see many adults today taking courses on very practical subjects, such as: time-management, improving relationships with people, developing personal commitment in career or profession, building better communication skills . . . the list goes on and on.

Prove this for yourself by asking yourself or a friend the following question:

"If you learned about time-management, communication skills, improving relationships and other topics like this in elementary and high school, do you think you would be generally more successful, effective or happy in life today?"

With the "WIN-WIN" Book, your young person will have the opportunity to develop these areas very easily and in a way that will make them feel good about their sport, their friends, their family, their education . . . about their life.

With this book, your young person will develop a very definite advantage in their life. They will be preparing for their future in a way that has never been available to young people. This book is a true gift to their life.

Dear Parent

Giving your opinion of The "WIN-WIN" Book will show your son or daughter that you are truly concerned about something that is important to them. This action will help them to be more initiating in their lives. If they ask you to read to them, to listen to them read, or to participate in some other way, your support will be a very meaningful and rewarding experience to them.

Dear Coach or Teacher

Giving your opinion of The "WIN-WIN" Book will show your young person that you are truly concerned about something that is important to them. As you know, this action will also help them to be more initiating in their lives. If they make any suggestions regarding the use of the book or any developmental idea, your support will be a very valuable experience.

*Finally, let's take a look
at your young athlete's development
and the part that The "WIN-WIN" Book
can play in it.*

This book is designed for your young athlete:

- ▶ to recognize the positive traits and qualities that they are learning through participation in their sport(s),
- ▶ to actively develop these positive traits and qualities in their sport,
- ▶ to be guided to bring these positive traits and qualities into their everyday lives,
- ▶ to be prepared to bring the positive traits and qualities into their future so they'll enjoy success and happiness in their young adult and adult lives.

With ongoing use of this book, your young person will internalize a system of principles that they can access to handle various common life situations and challenges. The topic index section of this book will give you an idea of the positive mindset your child or teen will be developing if they are encouraged to continue using this book throughout their involvement in youth sports. With this type of personal mindset, they'll be 'on top of their game' - able to see life experiences more objectively and use their life experiences to grow, to build confidence and character, and become generally more effective.

The lesson pages were developed from wide research on sports training, child and adolescent personal growth and development, case studies, interviews, and professional development and success/motivation principles.

Garo's Guidelines were developed directly from the personal issues and concerns of students (many of which were young athletes). Students from 100 schools (that Garo visited) participated in a program in which they shared their views on success, happiness, school, sports, family and other important areas of their lives. This open, honest portrayal of these young people's goals and concerns provided valuable information regarding the way they see the world. Using this information and Garo's actual experience in the world of sports, Garo's Guidelines were designed to be: 1) quick, easy and fun to read, 2) in language designed to appeal to young people, 3) results-oriented.

Dear Parent

This book is an exceptional developmental tool for your child or teenager. Every idea presented in this book supports your young's person's development of positive traits and social skills. You may want to consult with teachers and other youth development and education authorities and ask them how the book's content aligns with and supports youth development ideas available in their specific field. If they have questions, comments or suggestions, please write to us at:

The WIN-WIN Book
1244 Snyder Avenue
Suite 133
Phila. PA 19148

Dear Coach or Teacher,

If you see the merit of this book for today's youth, please use your influence to bring it into the hands of the young people whom you can directly or indirectly reach. For volunteer or income-earning opportunities, see page 20.

(We would like to acknowledge any noteworthy action in this area by thanking you in the Acknowledgments section of a future edition of the WIN-WIN Book.)

If you have made a contribution in this area or if you would like ideas on how to help our young people in this way, please write us at:

The WIN-WIN Book
1244 Snyder Avenue
Suite 133
Phila. PA 19148

Garo Yepremian

Garo Yepremian, born on June 2, 1944, in Larnaca, Cyprus began his remarkable journey to fame at age 16 when he moved to London, England. In England, he supported himself as a men's fabric salesman with the hope of someday attending college. He later moved to Indianapolis, Indiana, at the suggestion of his brother Krikor. He came, not with thoughts of great fame and fortune, but with the hope of a college scholarship by kicking something his brother called a 'football'.

Garo's only experience had been in soccer and he had almost no knowledge of American football. He began practicing but was disappointed to learn that his soccer background prevented him from collegiate competition, as ruled by the NCAA. This didn't stop Garo. He simply continued to practice kicking on a lot at Butler University. By good fortune, he was seen, discovered and signed by the NFL.

He was on his way, and played for the Detroit Lions, Miami Dolphins, New Orleans Saints, and Tampa Bay Buccaneers. From 1966 through 1981 he only missed one season - 1969 when he volunteered to serve in the US. army. Garo was voted Kicker of the Decade, 1970 -1980.

Garo genuinely cares for young people and is currently bringing his positive inspirational message to schools. He is also a nationally recognized motivational speaker for adult audiences around the country.

Garo's Record

1966 - 6 field goals in a single game/Lions v Minnesota
1966 - 4 field goals in a single quater
1971 - AFC leading scorer/117 points
1971 - 37 yard field goal to end longest game/82 minutes, 40 seconds
1972 - member of the undefeated Miami Dolphins
1974 - 5 field goals to win Pro Bowl for AFC.
 selected AFC All-Pro and MVP, 1974.
1979 - streak extended to 20 consecutive field goals without a miss
1980 - scored his 1,000th point and 200th field goal
1971, 1972, 1973 - played in three SuperBowls, scoring in all three for a total of 11 points.

Garo's "Golden Rules in the Sport of Life"

1. Begin each day thankful for your freedoms, faith, teachers and above all, family.
2. Believe in yourself (It's all right to like yourself).
3. Believe in your dreams (Who else can make them come true?)
4. Choose the right friends (Remember, a true friend will never hurt you).
5. Handle peer pressure by being true to your own values.
6. Set realistic goals (Goals that are important to you).
7. Always be positive (Strive to look on the bright side).
8. Treat all people with respect (Yes, sometimes it's hard, but you will be rewarded).
9. Listen to learn (Positive and unpleasant guidance are based on caring).
10. Be accountable and responsible for your actions (Strive to make the right decisions).
11. Maintain the proper values (Personal Integrity, Competence and Courage).
12. Be personally disciplined (It's tough, but necessary to avoid harmful habits).
13. Remember, you are the future (Positive team efforts will make it a bright one).

Anthony Rubbo

Like Garo Yepremian, Anthony Rubbo also has a special place in his heart for young people. In The "WIN-WIN" Book, he uses his motivational writing talent to present success ideas so that they can be very easily understood, enjoyed, and used by young athletes. He shows how true success is not only about winning the outer game, but also importantly about winning the *inner game* - the important game of ongoing total personal effort and steady improvement.

Anthony presents developmental ideas in a very special way - by relating them to something important in the reader's life. For example, in his book, *The Power of Personal Commitment*, he presents a way for adults to see how the many events and situations *in their career or profession* contribute to their personal development. In The "WIN-WIN" Book, Anthony presents a way for young athletes to see how events and situations *in their sport* contribute to their personal development.

The added benefit to the young athlete is that Anthony translates adult motivational ideas from his other books to language that makes sense to the child or teenager. Since career and profession are an important part of a person's life, he translates the most valuable ideas from his book on personal commitment to plant seeds in the young athlete's mind regarding their future.

He also brings in positive ideas regarding the different areas of a young person's life to provide a well-rounded approach to personal growth and social development.

His concern for young people is also evident in his hobby of songwriting. He wrote and produced the song, *Put The World In Their Hands*. The song is about opening opportunities for success and happiness for our young people. The song was performed on TV and won an award in the world's leading songwriting competition.

Including The "WIN-WIN" Book, Anthony has written four books on personal growth and development. He has also written a novel. He is the originator of the CAPE™ (Career and Personal Effectiveness) Program, a program tailored to specific needs and objectives of companies and organizations. The CAPE™ Program presents a *hands-on* way for adults in the work-force to see how the events and situations in their career or professional life contribute to their *personal* development.

Write to:

**Windom Publishing Co.
1244 Snyder Avenue
Suite 133
Philadelphia PA 19148**

*to correspond with the authors
or for information on the following:*

Opportunities for Teenagers and Young Adults

- Income-Earning Opportunities for Teenagers and Young Adults
- Volunteer Opportunities for Teenagers and Young Adults

Opportunities for Adults

- Income-Earning Opportunities for Adults
- Volunteer Opportunities for Adults

"WIN-WIN" Programs

- WIN-WIN Programs/Camps for Athletes and Students
- WIN-WIN Programs for Parents and Adults
- WIN-WIN Programs for Companies and Organizations

Garo Yepremian

- Garo Yepremian's Motivational Speaking Services
- Garo Yepremian Memorabilia

Anthony Rubbo

- Anthony Rubbo's CAPE™
  (Career and Personal Effectiveness) Program
  for Companies and Organizations
- Anthony Rubbo's Motivational Speaking Services

*If you are writing about volunteer or income-earning
opportunities, please include a letter and/or resume.*

CHAPTER INDEX

PRACTICE

1. When you play with feeling
2. When you are practicing your sport 'for you'
3. When you are learning your fundamentals
4. When you practice regularly
5. When you keep your fundamentals sharp
6. When you recognize your natural talent
7. When you bring the spirit of competition into your practice
8. When learning a new skill feels uncomfortable
9. When you work hard to turn a weakness into a strength
10. When you are on time for practice and for games
11. When you don't feel like practicing and you go anyway
12. When you fully enjoy practicing

THE GAME

13. When you are confident while you are playing
14. When you are doing well and your team is not
15. When you warm up
16. When you are not doing well and your team is
17. When you are sure of victory
18. When you think the other team is better than your team
19. When you hear the crowds
20. When you make an error
21. When a bad call is made
22. When you're not playing in a game

AFTER THE GAME

23. When you win
24. When you 'high-five' the other team
25. When you receive an award

26. When an MVP is chosen
27. When you review your game
28. When you use this book
29. When you lose a game

PROGRESS/ADVANCEMENT

30. When you set goals
31. When you set long-range goals
32. When you manage your time

33. When you imagine a successful performance
34. When you've reached a new performance level
35. When you have an obstacle

36. When you have a set-back
37. When you feel stressed
38. When you feel like quitting

COACHING

39. When you follow your coach's instructions
40. When you are corrected by your coach
41. When you share feelings with your coach

42. When you are coached by older players
43. When you coach someone

LEARNING ABOUT YOUR SPORT

44. When you use TV to learn about your sport
45. When you learn 'from yourself'
46. When you follow a team or a player

47. When you learn about your sport from people
48. When you read about your sport

REACHING YOUR POTENTIAL

49. When you 'play hard' at your sport
50. When you are 'in the moment'
51. When you expect the best from yourself

52. When you work on a good habit
53. When you have positive pride
54. When you work on removing a bad habit

PHYSICAL HEALTH AND FITNESS

55. When you eat the right foods
56. When you exercise or condition
57. When you get a good night's sleep

58. When you feel good *naturally*
59. When you make time for relaxation

PEOPLE

60. When you look for the good in people
61. When you expect the best from others
62. When you help someone

63. When you are being helped by someone
64. When you 'buddy' with someone for success
65. When you forgive someone

66. When you handle peer pressure
67. When you have a problem with someone
68. When you have a problem with your parents

69. When you are being 'psyched out'
70. When you see people behaving badly
71. When you work well with others

CHARACTER

72. When you are optimistic
73. When you are tough
74. When you are humble in your accomplishments

75. When you are confident in the face of doubt
76. When you are courageous in competition
77. When you play by the rules

78. When you are 'cool'
79. When you feel the urge to get angry
80. When you allow yourself to be forgiven
81. When you 'go for it' and handle challenges <u>now</u>